GREEN DIAMONDS

The Pleasures and Profits of Investing in Minor-League Baseball

JAY ACTON
WITH
NICK BAKALAR

ZEBRA BOOKS
KENSINGTON PUBLISHING CORP.

ZEBRA BOOKS

are published by

Kensington Publishing Corp.
475 Park Avenue South
New York, NY 10016

First Printing: May, 1993

Printed in the United States of America

ISBN 0-8217-4150-0

Library of Congress Catalog Card Number: 93-077356

Dedication

For Rose, Bobby, and Elizabeth
—J.A.

For Francine and Elizabeth
—N.B.

ACKNOWLEDGMENTS

The authors would like to thank the following people for taking time to speak with us about baseball and business: Dave Baggott, Dennis Bastien, Rita Baxter, Bill Blackwell, Frank Boulton, Dave Carl, Scott Carter, Bill Davidson, Rich Hill, Arthur Hittner, Richard Holtzman, John Isherwood, Peter Kirk, Bill Larsen, Mary LeBlanc, Alan Levin, Bob Linyard, Keith Lupton, Eric Margenau, Bob Miller (National Association office), Leanne Pagliai, Jenni Parmalee, Jim Paul, Craig Pletenik, Steve Resnick, Bob Richmond, Rip Rowan, Steve Shaad, Brian Silverman, Craig Stein, John Thorn, John Tull, and Miles Wolff.

The media-relations departments of every team we called, both major-league and minor-league were unfailingly helpful. The people who helped us in those offices go unmentioned here, but their contributions were enormous.

TABLE OF CONTENTS

TABLE OF CONTENTS

Table of Contents

PREFACE

Last year, the Buffalo Bisons had higher attendance than three major-league teams. Two new leagues will be set up this year, each with about six new teams. There are minor-league teams now in more than 150 towns and cities across America and in Canada. Caribbean and Mexican leagues flourish in the winter. Chattanooga Lookouts caps, Toledo Mud Hens jerseys, and Durham Bulls T-shirts are high style in high schools and colleges across the country. New stadiums are built every year that house minor-league teams in a style that used to be reserved for the Bigs. More people than ever are going to minor-league baseball games.

The parallel development—and I won't try to sort out cause and effect here—is that minor-league teams are being run more professionally, by marketing, sales, and baseball experts who know how to develop and operate a successful business. If it was once true that the typical bush league team was run by someone who had a "real" job the rest of the year, and just opened the gates of a rundown ball field in the spring to make a couple of bucks selling peanuts and beer, it's not true anymore.

At the same time, the old-fashioned charm of the minors persists—and this is really what fans want and what minor-league operators are selling. If the typical major-league stadium these days is thirty million tons of concrete and plastic grass in the middle of a fourteen-acre parking lot, a minor-league park is a place where everyone can sit near a real grass field and overhear the manager talking to his pitcher in the dugout. Players—even the stars—still run out ground balls and stay after the game to sign autographs. Owners walk through the stands during games, and know their regular customers by name. And a family of four can spend the afternoon at a professional baseball game—including hot dogs, beer, and a souvenir—for about the price of two seats up the right field line in Dodger Stadium.

So this book is about more than investing in a business—it's also about a place—the minor leagues—where you can experience again the joy of baseball you felt when you first noticed there was such a game: pure, natural baseball, nothing artificial added.

PART ONE

Sports as Business

1

The Dream of Owning a Team

If a person has some money to invest—and I'm talking about regular people here, not movie stars or presidents of automobile companies—there are all sorts of investments you can try, from common stocks and bank certificates of deposits to government securities to stock options and commodities if you want to get fancy. And within these choices is, of course, the entire range of American (and for that matter foreign) industry. Sometimes you make money on these investments, sometimes they don't work out so well. Some of these are risky, some not so. And there are plenty of experts—and plenty of books—to tell you what you should do with your investment dollar, and where you're going to make the most, the fastest.

Like those other books, this is a book about making

money. I don't invest in minor-league baseball teams because I have money to burn. First, I don't have money to burn. And even if I did, I'm not the type to burn it. So don't get the idea that investing in baseball is the same as going to the track or buying a lottery ticket. It's not. It has its risks—greater risks than a lot of investments, less than others—but if you understand how it works, it has its financial rewards as well. And that's what this book is about: understanding how minor-league baseball works, so that you can invest in it wisely.

You wouldn't have picked up this book if you weren't at least a little bit of a baseball fan. Of course, you're a grown-up now, and you don't have batting averages memorized the way you used to, and your mother tossed out your baseball-card collection years ago, and artificial turf and designated hitters are really annoying, and if your baseball consciousness goes back far enough, you probably still believe that two eight-team leagues are an integral element of the music of the heavenly spheres. It's not the way it used to be, and blah, blah, blah. But let's face it—when spring comes, you still think that this is your team's year, and even when it turns out not to be, the games on TV still nag at your attention even when you've got more important things to do, and when you're driving around in the car with the radio on, a baseball game is really the only thing worth listening to. You follow other sports—football fills some time in the fall, and basketball's entertaining, even though the college game these days seems more interesting than the NBA, and you may have even developed a taste for hockey—depending on where you live—or for some more exotic sport—say, lacrosse, if you happened to have gone to a school where they play it. But you know that none of these is ever going to replace baseball as your central idea of what a sport is supposed to be. So investing in baseball is always going to be affected by some persistent dream left over from childhood—of getting into the game, being part of the team, making the crucial play. Baseball is a business, but no matter how many profit-and-loss statements you read—and I've read a lot of them—it's still a game, the best game there is. Emotionally, it's just not the same as other investments. When you put money in baseball, it's not the same as putting it in Treasury bills. But—to come back to earth here for a second— that doesn't mean you have to lose money doing it.

As recently as 1974, my friend Bob Ryan could write in his book about the minor leagues called *Wait Till I Make the Show* "Why would anyone want to write a book about the minor leagues? They are dead, or at least dying. They are an anachronism, a relic of a simpler age." Yet fifteen years later, minor-league teams—A-league teams, no less—were selling for more than $4 million.

Times, obviously, have changed, and in fact, there are good and sensible reasons to invest in minor-league baseball, even apart from sentimental ones: in 1991, more than twenty-six million people paid to see minor-league teams play ball—a 5% increase over the previous year. In twelve different leagues, attendance records were set, and there wasn't a single league that drew fewer than a million fans. The Buffalo Bisons alone drew 1,188,972, a new record for a minor-league team. In a time when the price of tickets, beer, and hot dogs for a family of four at a major-league baseball game comes to somewhere around $85—well, let's just say that there are good reasons why people want to watch the farm teams play ball. There are minor-league teams in more than 150 communities—a vast national market that has made quite a few people quite a bit of money.

In 1981, a group of investors headed by a professor at the University of Massachusetts bought the Holyoke Millers, a Double-A team, for $85,000. After a couple of moves and a couple of name changes, Professor Jerome Mileur now heads the Harrisburg Senators, a Montreal Expos affiliate, and the team is worth well over $3 million today. Miles Wolff bought the Durham Bulls in 1981 for $2,500 and sold the team, ten years and one Hollywood movie later, for $4 million. During the same period of time, some minor-league teams lost money and some had substantial operating profits. When you're finished reading this book, you'll have an idea of why some teams flourish and others don't, you'll understand the risks, you'll have some basis on which to make judgments, and, if in the end you decide to put some money in play, you'll be going into the investment with your eyes wide open.

Even if in the end you decide that investing in baseball is not something you want to do, you'll learn in this book how minor-league teams work, how they are advertised and promoted, where they obtain their income, how they relate to the major-league affiliates, how they succeed, and how they fail. I'll warn you at the outset that a minor-league baseball team is not the right place to put your life savings, but I'll also show you how you can make an investment, see it grow, and have some fun in the bargain. I'll introduce you to some of the people who run this business and play this game. I'll teach you what I've learned from my own experiences and those of other owners. Finally, I hope I can convey some of the joy of working in this business, and show you how you can share in it.

2

Business and Psychology

I didn't get started in investing in minor-league baseball by reading the *Wall Street Journal* or talking to
my stockbroker. I've made some money in publishing—I'm a literary agent—and I've made enough to
have a little extra to invest. By the early 1980s, I'd
invested in quite a few things, most of them pretty
conventional—like stocks and real estate. Most of my
investments have paid off—no one who writes a book
on investing ever admits that some investments
didn't pay off so well, but I'll break with that tradition
here by saying that some of them worked better than
others. But my money was put in the kinds of places
your father would tell you to put money if you have
some extra: reliable stocks, government securities, a
little bit in more risky ventures, and all diversified
enough to keep my eggs in a number of different

baskets. I certainly never thought of myself as the kind of guy who invests in trendy night clubs, Broadway shows, or deep-sea treasure hunts—and I still don't think of myself that way.

For the kind of investor I am, minor-league baseball seems, at best, a bit of a stretch. But I got involved in it quite naturally through my primary occupation. One of my clients was Roger Kahn—anyone who's reading this book probably doesn't need to be told who he is, but just for the record, he's the author of *The Boys of Summer,* probably one of the best books on baseball—or any other sport for that matter—ever written. He's also written a number of other books, both fiction and nonfiction, including a terrific book about minor-league baseball called *Good Enough to Dream.* We sold Roger's proposal for that book to Doubleday in 1983 and Roger and I used some of the money from the advance to buy an interest in a Class-A team called the Utica Blue Sox. Roger was doing this for lots of reasons, none of them having much to do with making money. Of course, he makes his money by writing, and he wanted to write about the minors. And he figured that owning a minor-league team would be the best possible way to learn about life on the farm. So I guess you could say that he was in it for the money, in a sense.

But there's more to it than that. Roger doesn't have to buy a minor-league team in order to find a subject for a book. But like me—and probably you—Roger is a fan. He dreamed of being involved in the game. And this was a splendid way to fulfill that dream.

We had started out thinking about a book on managers or coaches or owners—an inside baseball story.

But then we decided that we had some ideas about how a team should be run, so why not just show them how it's done? Roger knew Johnny Johnson, who was President of the National Association (the governing body of the minor leagues) at the time, and he agreed to make some inquiries on our behalf. Eventually, he put us in touch with Miles Wolff, who was the first to suggest that the Utica team was the one to buy. (Miles is the publisher of *Baseball America,* the Bible of the minor leagues, and the former owner of the Durham Bulls. I'll tell you more about him later.)

Utica had no affiliation with a major-league club. Their park was terrible. The previous owner had neglected to pay the electric bill, so we had to pay that before the electric company would agree to turn on the lights for us. The team cost $15,000 and the deal was so informal that we weren't even quite sure who we were buying it from. Essentially, Miles took care of the deal, and we went along with it. But it turned out to be exactly what we hoped it would be. That first season we didn't make any money, but we didn't lose any either. And our team won the championship, beating out the Orioles in a two out of three postseason series. It wasn't an investment, and it wasn't work—it was fun.

And that's where it started for me—not with advice from an investment company, but with a writer, a book, and a dream. This was not a cold piece of investing for any of us, not just another way to diversify a portfolio, not just a place to stick a little extra money when you're feeling flush. When you put money in this game, your heart is in it too.

How much money do you need?

The short answer is, more than you used to. In the early 1980s, teams were being sold for as little as $10,000, but those days are gone. Of course, the amount of money you invest can vary widely. As you will see, a controlling interest in a full-season team can run into seven figures. On the low end—if you're willing to do some diligent research—there may still be opportunities to purchase stock for as little as $1,000. However, there is no McDonald's of Minor-League Baseball where you can walk right up to the window and order $1,000 of stock. You'll have to do some sleuthing. Part of your search may involve identifying original stockholders from teams formed in the 1950s and 1960s. Some of these stockholders may have died, moved, or otherwise no longer be "active" stockholders. When I say "active" I mean they or their heirs may not realize they still have the stock. They may be happy to have someone take it off their hands for a relatively nominal amount.

So where do you look for such stockholder names? Try corporate records that may be on file with your state's Secretary of State. Try firms that track missing stockholders. You can also get anecdotal evidence of ownership through local newspaper accounts. Or go to the city or town you're interested in and visit the sports editor of the local paper, or the head of the local stadium authority or parks department. You'll probably find some interesting municipal history, and you may come across that little treasure trove of stock you're looking for!

Now back to the business of buying whole teams.

In very rough figures, here's how I would estimate the value of teams in the various classes of minor-league ball (we'll get into the meaning of these divisions later—it's enough for now to say that these classes indicate the level of skill of the players).

Rookie-league teams. For the ones that can be bought and sold, the price is around $500,000, but many of these teams in the Gulf Coast League, the Arizona League, the Pioneer League, and the Appalachian League, are run by major-league teams, and are not for sale.

Short-season A teams. These teams are in the New York-Penn League and the Northwest League, with locations like Elmira, New York and Boise, Idaho. They're worth a minimum of $500,000.

Full-season A teams. These play in the Carolina League, the Florida State League, the Midwest League, and the South Atlantic League. They're going for in excess of $1 million. There are exceptions—like the Durham Bulls, for example—but we'll get to that later.

Double-A teams. Now we're getting up there. The leagues these teams play in—the Texas League, the Southern League, and the Eastern League—include some of the most famous teams in the minors like the Memphis Chicks. These are worth in the neighborhood of $3.5 million.

Triple-A teams. Best in the minors—these have the players most likely to spend part of the season—or the rest of their careers—in the Show. And the teams they play for include some of the biggest money-makers in baseball: the Buffalo Bisons, the Columbus

Clippers, the Nashville Sounds. You can't own the whole team here for less than $5 million.

According to Miles Wolff, all this started in the mid-1970s. Pat McKernan, who owned the Pittsfield franchise at the time, put it up for sale among his baseball colleagues for $10,000. Everyone thought he was nuts, and he had no takers. So he put an ad in the *Wall Street Journal*, saying that he had a minor-league team for sale for $40,000. He immediately got more offers than he knew what to do with. This was a revelation for everyone in the minors at the time. There were people outside of baseball willing to pay enormous amounts of money to own minor-league teams. Now, Wolff says, the prices of teams tend to be pegged to the best and most profitable team in the league: just as a business proposition, Durham is probably worth the $4 million it sold for, but every other team in the league is worth proportionately more now because of that sale—and that includes a lot of teams that aren't making much money.

Now this doesn't mean that you need to be Warren Buffet to make an investment (yes, he did buy a team: the Omaha Royals in the American Association), so don't throw up your hands yet. There are ways to get in for much less than the cost of buying the whole team.

How ownership deals work

Frank Boulton was an owner of the Prince William Cannons, a New York Yankees Class-A affiliate, and one of the best-run and most profitable teams in the minors. He bought the team with some partners for $1.3 million in 1988—the first minor-league team he'd ever been involved with. This seemed like a lot of money at the time, especially for a team that wasn't making a nickel. But Boulton saw the potential, and jumped on it. Today, the team makes a 30% return on investment—spectacular in any industry, practically unheard of in minor-league baseball.

Boulton is a banker by trade who was a vice-president of UBS Securities, and one of the founders of their mortgage-backed securities group. He came to the baseball business with a few qualifications. First, he's an experienced dealmaker—he's made deals for everything from real estate to Holstein cows, and he knows his way around the financial world. And— always a prerequisite—he's a fan. A serious athlete himself—he was recruited by a slew of colleges to play football, but an injury in his freshman year ended his playing days—he's been a player and a fan all his life.

The Prince William Cannons were set up as a stock corporation. Boulton and Arthur Silber, who is chairman of the Sterling Bank and Trust Co. in Baltimore when he's not wearing his baseball cap, were the majority stockholders. Silber was Chairman and Boulton was the President of the corporation. Silber and Boulton are in charge of the daily operation of the team, just as the heads of any other corporation would be in charge of their business. But there are many variations in the way ownership deals are structured.

Boulton sold his interest in the Cannons in October, 1992. Then in November, 1992, along with Buddy

Harrelson, the former New York Mets shortstop and manager, he bought the Peninsula Pilots from me and my partner Eric Margenau. He moved them to Wilmington Delaware, where they will be known as the Wilmington Blue Rocks. This team will be set up as a partnership, but there's more to this than finding a few investors who have $50,000 apiece—that's the minimum price to get in on this deal.

When you transfer the controlling interest of a team, there are plenty of people who have something to say about it. First, you need approval from the league. The other owners want to know who they're going to be dealing with, and they have a right to approve the investors who are joining their system. Then the National Association of Professional Baseball Leagues has to give approval. And finally the major leagues have to give their okay—they want to know where their affiliates are going, and why.

Getting the approval of the National Association is complex. Major-league Rule 36 (I'll tell you all about this in detail in Chapter 7) requires that all transactions be reviewed by the President of the NAPBL so that he can determine whether the transaction constitutes a transfer of control interest. There are a slew of documents the President has to see—stock purchase or sales agreements, private placement memoranda, shareholders' agreements, collateral assignments—every piece of paper a lawyer can invent has to be turned over to the President. He even gets to see broadcasting agreements and concession contracts.

It is now against the rules of baseball to pledge your franchise or its territorial rights as security for a loan. Franchises are required to maintain debt-equity ratios of 45% to 55%—arrived at by a formula that would confuse even a C.P.A.

The President must know who is getting into the business, so he needs to have biographical information along with releases sufficient for him to conduct an investigation of the individuals concerned. He requires balance sheets and a list of all officers of any business enterprise that is buying the club, and personal financial statements from any individual who will own more than 5% of the team. In the end, any transaction can be vetoed by the League, the President of the National Association, or the Commissioner of Baseball. And the process requires a $5,000 nonrefundable processing fee to cover the investigation.

In the case of the Wilmington operation, Boulton got the city to agree to build a new $7 million facility—part city funds, part state, and part private—for his team in a city that hasn't had professional baseball since 1952.

Buddy Harrelson owns a piece of the Blue Rocks. He's also a general partner, responsible for the day-to-day running of the franchise. The Wilmington deal has Bud and Frank as general partners, and a dozen or so limited partners. Even at $50,000 apiece, Boulton has more people asking for shares than he has shares to sell. From Boulton's point of view, this is the best way to do it. The limited partners make an investment—their liability is limited to the amount they've put in. And the general partners—who function as limited partners at the same time, so that their own money is in the pot—have responsibility for and ultimate control over the operation. The limited partners in the Harrelson deal won't be making decisions about how to run the business—they're going to be leaving that to the experts. Boulton welcomes their participation—he views them as ambassadors to the city, and very important people to the club. Local ownership is particularly important to Boulton. But he wants to leave the running of the club to the people who know how to do it.

There are no guarantees in any business, but Boulton is serious about making money. This is not play money, it's not a hobby for rich people, and it's not an elaborate tax dodge—those days are gone. Minor-league baseball is a money-making business when you do it right, and Boulton is determined to see his investors make money. So if the limited partners are thinking of sitting in the dugout and calling plays—well, that's just a fantasy. And, as Boulton will tell you if you catch him in an unguarded moment, some limited partners have some pretty strange fantasies.

Boulton's deal in Wilmington puts quite a bit of money at risk, too. He has sold fifty units at $50,000 each: a $2.5 million deal. The team will cost $1.6 million to buy from its present owners. He'll spend $50,000 in legal fees—yes, the lawyers will get their share of any deal. Then he'll spend $750,000 on furnishing the stadium that Wilmington will build. He'll buy the scoreboard. He'll install the public-address system. He'll buy the concession stands and put in the hot-dog grills, soda fountains, and beer dispensers. He'll buy the rakes and lawnmowers, the wheelbarrows and landscaping tools, the machines to draw the baselines—everything you need to maintain a professional-quality playing field. He'll buy all the furniture for the offices and the skyboxes. When all that's done, he'll have $100,000 left as working capital for the franchise. Then he'll lease the stadium from the city of Wilmington—and pay for maintenance all year round, including the salaries of everyone who works there, so that the city can use it when the Blue Rocks aren't at home. The Blue Rocks will pay the entire cost of running the stadium—the city pays nothing after building it. There's plenty of room for subjective judgment in matters of government spending, especially these days, but for the money they're putting into it, it may not be a bad deal at all for Delaware and the city of Wilmington.

When a baseball team starts negotiating with a city or country government, the team is at a considerable advantage. The National Association of Professional Baseball Leagues—divides up the country into territories. Generally, no two teams can be based in the same territory. So when Wilmington started talking to the Peninsula Pilots about moving the team there, the Pilots were the only game in town. No other team was allowed even to discuss moving there.

The appeal for Wilmington was that the stadium would be multipurpose. The team will play there sixty or seventy days a year. The rest of the time, the stadium belongs to the city for whatever they want to use it for—school sports events, high-school or college graduations, concerts. Delaware had no decent facility for such things, so this added considerably to the appeal of the deal.

Boulton is involved in other deals as well. He bought the Albany-Colonie Yankees, an AA affiliate in

Albany, and he wants to move them to Suffolk County, Long Island. He and the county are discussing building a multipurpose stadium to house the team there.

Do you have to be a high-roller, or can this be considered an ordinary businessman's deal?

There was a time when you would have to be pretty daring to invest in a minor-league baseball team. Teams came and went, a lot of them didn't make much money—if they made any at all—and they were run on a less-than-professional level. There are still some pretty poorly run teams in some pretty bad locations that are probably not very good investments. But if you're involved with a modern, well-run minor-league team—and there are quite a few of these—you've put your money where you can expect a return at least as high as you would get in any other well-run business.

During the 1980s there was a big run-up in the price of minor-league teams, and that money—the money made as teams were appreciating quickly—has probably already been made. My guess is that most of the people investing in teams in those days had no idea how much they'd later be worth. Investing in the minors became chic in the 1980s—lots of show-business people and other celebrities got involved—and the prices were driven up by that demand. Who could have guessed that the Harrisburg Senators, an AA team in the Eastern League which sold in 1980 for $85,000, would be worth more than

$3 million a decade later? Baseball teams broker Bob Richmond reminded me that the Eugene Emeralds—they're now the Triple-A Edmonton Trappers in the Pacific Coast League—sold for $8,000 in 1973 to a group of investors who called themselves "The Trembling 20." The Trappers today are one of the premier teams in the minors, and the franchise is probably worth more than $5 million. In Chapter 4, I'll talk more about which teams and which markets are likely to be the best over the coming years, and I'll try to explain why. For now, let's just say that you have to look for teams that are run well as businesses, that produce a cash flow and net profits, and that have a clear future as a going concern.

And you have to be aware of risks. Many ordinary businesses sell at five to ten times earnings, which is about where most minor-league teams would fall. But there are teams selling at up to fifteen times their earnings, which makes you wonder if they're really worth what people are paying for them. And there are risks special to baseball that you have to know about before you put your money down.

For example, the major-league affiliations of teams can change, and the minor-league team has little control over this. The Peoria Chiefs, a Class-A team in the Midwest League, had an affiliation with the Chicago Cubs—perfect for their location in the heart of Cubs country. But then the Cubs bought the Rockford team in the same league—which used to be a Montreal Expos affiliate. Rockford, of course, is also the home of plenty of Cubs fans, and the league objected on the grounds that this wasn't fair to Peoria. The Cubs say they're going to stock both teams with players. But what if they change their minds and decide to sign players to only one of these two teams? What happens to your investment in Peoria if the major-league team decides that Rockford is the only team they need? These are some of the real risks that minor-league teams run, and any investor has to face them.

Minor-league teams vary quite a bit in their financial stability, and some are just plain overvalued, even allowing for intangibles like fan loyalty or the number of people you see walking around in their T-shirts. I once considered buying a team—a confidentiality agreement prevents me from saying which one—that looked terrific from the outside. The owner claimed the franchise had a cash flow of over a million dollars a year. But when you took a closer look, the actual cash flow was more like $500,000 a year once you subtracted various expenses that he wasn't counting. Another team I looked into was a stock corporation that had been set up in the 1950s so informally that after a reverse stock split some years ago, they didn't even know who all the shareholders were. About a fifth of them had just disappeared. When my partners and I tried to escrow 20% of the money to cover these people, the deal fell through. But what if they had appeared at some point, claiming that the team was worth more than it was sold for? The buyer would be buying not only a baseball team, but a colossal lawsuit as well.

The PBA—the Professional Baseball Agreement—runs through 1997, but it is open for renegotiation in 1994. No one knows what that negotiation is going to mean for the minor leagues. Major-league baseball has its own problems at the moment. Numerous teams are for sale. The TV money seems to have reached the top, and is headed down. Player salaries, as everyone knows, are sky-high, and, although attendance is still holding up pretty well in most places, some teams are beginning to have trouble filling up seats. All this will make the major-league teams take a very hard look at their minor-league affiliates, both those that are successful and those that aren't.

Are you emotionally right for this kind of investment?

Bob Richmond probably knows more than anyone about how these investments work and how deals are put together. In fact, if you're seriously interested, he's probably one of the first people you should be talking to. First, Richmond is a baseball man. He's been in minor-league ball in various capacities for more than twenty of his fifty-one years. Today, he's co-owner of the Midland Angels in the Texas League, and he's President of the Class-A Northwest League. His first job in the business was as legal counsel for the Eugene Emeralds, at that time a team in the Pacific Coast League. He took over the team—I'll use his words—"because they couldn't find anyone else dumb enough to do it." Richmond is an easygoing guy with a self-deprecatory sense of humor, but I think there's a psychological truth hidden in that remark that bears examination. The fact is that if you're interested in making a fast, high return on your money, or if you're interested in seeing robust growth in your investment, or if you're interested in a secure place to put your money for retirement—if any of those reasons are what lies behind your investment, you should probably be looking for a good CD or a tax-free municipal bond and just forget about baseball.

Richmond lived through the years when all it required to own a team was—as he put it in a recent conversation—"a Visa card and a warm body." When he was first in the business, teams didn't make much money, and couldn't lose much. Most were run on a shoestring by locals who just wanted to have some baseball in their communities. They weren't looking to make piles of money, they weren't looking to sell out to Wall Street types, they weren't interested in moving the team to a better ballpark in a bigger city. I don't want to engage in a lot of teary-eyed nostalgia about the good old days—some parts of minor-league ball in those days weren't all that good—but it's not too much to say that motivations in these matters have changed quite a bit over the past ten or fifteen years.

Back in the early 1970s, Richmond recalls, ownership was a sometime thing. He was president of the Northwest League at that time, and one of the owners called him up in the middle of the season to tell him that he was quitting. Richmond said get out of here, you can't quit, you own the team, it's the middle of the season, you can't walk off the field in the fifth inning unless it's raining, which it isn't, and you've got a schedule of games to play, and the guy said something like, oh yeah, just watch me. So Richmond had to drop everything to run down and try to put together a cooperative to keep the franchise afloat for another year. Needless to say, this is not the way it works today.

Bob Richmond is a good example of the kind of investor who is psychologically right for minor-league ball. He's done fine for himself in recent years, but when he started working in minor-league ball, it must have been for something other than the money. And he has an acute awareness of the uncertainties of the business even in these good times. He's a lawyer, so he could make a living in lots of other ways, but he stays in baseball because he loves the game. And you get the feeling, talking to him, that he'd stay in the game whether it made him rich or not. True, he's a businessman, and a good one, so he's in it for the money—but if there wasn't any money in it, he'd be in it anyway.

The future of minor-league baseball

There's an old saw that "baseball is less than a business, but more than a game." But if you're putting real money in this game, you want to have some pretty good idea of where the business is heading. Bob Richmond thinks of himself as a conservative investor. He's looking for people with discretionary income who love baseball and want to be a part of it. By his own admission, he's not a salesman. He talks to people, gives them the facts as he sees them, and lets them make their own decision about what to do with their money. He feels there are some people this investment just doesn't make sense for, and when he feels that way, he'll tell you. To be in this, you need a certain amount of money, you have to understand marketing, have good business sense, devote some time to watching and learning what's going on, and you have to love the game.

I'm trying to create a realistic picture, so I told you a little about what I see as the downside earlier in this chapter. But there's an upside, too, and in many ways, as a pure business investment, the minor leagues hold promise. With the Colorado Rockies and the Miami Marlins coming into the National League next year, the minors are going to have to expand to begin supplying the talent for the new franchises. The city of Bend, Oregon now has a Rockies Class-A affiliate in the Northwest League—a team that used to be one of the few independent operations—and the Rockies will share a rookie Arizona-League team with the Chicago Cubs. The Marlins have a Class-A affiliation in the New York-Penn League with the Elmira Pioneers, and they've set up a rookie affiliate as well.

The Player Development Contract (and we'll talk more about this in Chapter 3) has lots of problems as far as the relationship with the majors is concerned, but it does at least prevent some of the more whimsical practices of the past—there are now legally enforceable agreements in place that require that the majors to stock teams with players, pay certain expenses, and not abandon them without due process. In the old days, affiliations with major-league teams came and went—and as a result so did the minor-league teams themselves. Whatever the results of the negotiations for the new agreement next year, there will be support for the minor leagues from the bigs that will make it possible for minor league owners to do better than just break even.

While the minors have followed the healthy financial results of the majors over the past decade, they are in some ways in a better position now than their parent clubs. They provide a good show for a reasonable price, and the fans are responding in record numbers. There isn't any indication right now that attendance figures will decline over the next few years, and for many teams, they'll likely go up. Management is more professional than ever—the old baseball hands have been joined by sophisticated investors and businessmen, and the combination seems to be working well for many franchises. Maybe some of the old charm is gone, but so is some of the uncertainty. The old organizations produced lots of great anecdotes, but the new organizations are now producing better baseball and a better show for the fans, and more money for their owners and their municipalities.

PART TWO

The Real World of Minor-League Baseball

3

The Structure of the Minor Leagues

There are more than 150 minor-league teams in the U.S. and Canada, not counting the teams that play in Mexico and the Dominican Republic. They're spread all over the country—in thirty-seven different states. All of the leagues belong to an umbrella organization called the National Association of Professional Baseball Leagues, and almost every team has a major-league affiliate.

The National Association of Professional Baseball Leagues

Over its history, the National Association has had teams in every one of the fifty states except Alaska. During the ninety-one years of its existence, there have been 1,200 different cities and towns that have had minor-league teams. But never in its history has minor-league baseball thrived like it does today.

There are 5,500 players active now in the minors, and about 1,500 new ones are signed every year. Except for those on a handful of independent teams, all of these players, plus all the coaches and managers, are paid by the major-league affiliate team. In other words, the major-league team owns all the contracts, and can do with them what it likes. It assigns players, coaches, and managers, it moves them up to the majors and back down again. The minor-league management has no say over which players will play for them—they don't trade players, they don't sign contracts with them. The same goes for coaches and managers. Every one of them is assigned and paid by the major-league team.

The various minor leagues are bound together by a document called the National Association Agreement. The document outlines four objectives for the minor leagues: to perpetuate baseball by promoting the sport in the U.S. and internationally, to provide baseball at affordable prices, to promote and protect the interests of the leagues that operate under the agreement, and to maintain good relations with the major leagues.

The Association has a board of trustees, consisting of one representative from each member league, which raises funds and approves rule changes. The president is elected for a four-year term by a three-quarters vote of the membership.

Among other things, the National Association adjudicates disputes among the members and enforces the rules of the organization. It is empowered to levy fines and impose other kinds of sanctions on teams or leagues for rule violations. Membership in the Association guarantees a league control over its territory, and the Association specifies the terms of that control.

The Agreement includes, of course, a clause identical to the Major-League Rule 21, which is entitled "Conduct not in the Best Interests of Baseball"—a phrase that keeps turning up on the sports pages these days with all the commotion in the Office of the Commissioner of Baseball. This covers things like failing to give one's best effort to win (or making arrangements to lose), betting on games, giving gifts to umpires, and other such acts of malfeasance. These acts can result in one's being permanently banned from baseball, as some people have learned to their chagrin. So that no one concerned will forget where baseball stands on matters like this, a copy of this section has to be posted in the clubhouse of every minor-league team, just as it is posted in the clubhouse of every team in the majors.

The Agreement also lays out some rules of play. It specifies that these teams play by major-league rules, that you can't have stuff like tripleheaders (which used to be a feature of minor-league parks, usually after a couple of rainouts), and that interleague play is under the jurisdiction of the President of the National Association.

The As, the AAs, and the AAAs

Every major-league team now has one Triple-A and one Double-A affiliate. At the A and rookie-league levels, the number of affiliates varies, and it is here that you begin to see the difference between the player development philosophies of the different major-league teams.

In my view, a major-league team should have as many minor-league teams operating as possible. In order to have enough major-league talent available at all times, a team needs hundreds of players in varying stages of development. With the advent of free agency a major-league team has to consider that every position has to be replaced every six years, so you need people coming up all the time, ready to take over the major-league slot when the time comes. Branch Rickey, who really invented the farm system, used to have hundreds of players coming to spring training—he knew that the only way to get quality was to start with plenty of quantity.

Triple-A and Double-A are, of course, the last way-station for those few players who will make it to the majors, and the levels of competition in these leagues are near major-league quality. By the time you get down to A teams, though, quality can be harder to come by. There are even gradations—though not officially—between various A leagues. The Carolina League, for example, is considered a bit faster than the Midwest League, and the term "Advanced A," is used.

Following a period during which minor-league teams were disappearing rapidly, the numbers began to increase again in the 1980s. One of the reasons for this may have been the knowledge that the National League would expand, and that all of the teams would have to contribute players to those new teams. Some years ago Gordon Goldsberry, who was then the Chicago Cubs' VP for Minor Leagues and Scouting said: "When expansion comes, and all of the existing major-league clubs have to contribute to the expansion pool, we want to be ready—every team will need a surplus of talent, and we'll have it." The Cardinals have followed the same philosophy—they now have in addition to their Triple-A and Double-A teams, no fewer than four Class-A teams, and two rookie-classification franchises. Not all teams carry this many. The Pirates, for example, have only three Class-A teams and one rookie-league team. If you look in the paper, you'll see that the number of minor-league teams does not necessarily correlate with the place in the standings at the end of the season, but the aim is always a steady supply of major-league talent.

The relationship with the major leagues

The National Association and the major leagues function under an agreement called the Professional Baseball Agreement, which runs through 1997. This outlines the responsibilities of each of the organizations in relation to the functioning of the minor-league teams. Needless to say, the relationship between the majors and the minors is not without its rough spots. As it stands now, the major leagues take as much as 5% of the income of the minor-league affiliates to cover at least some of their expenses.

The major-league affiliate

The Salt Lake City Trappers, which I'll tell you more about in Chapter 10, are one of the few independent teams in the minors. By this I mean they have no major-league affiliate. For most teams this would be impossible—they couldn't sustain themselves as economic enterprises without the contribution of the parent team. Independent teams are willing to search the world—literally—for major-league sponsorship. One independent team, the Salinas Spurs in the Class-A California League, unable to find an American major-league sponsor, signed a deal with the Nankai Hawks and the Yakult Swallows in the Japanese League to provide talent for their teams.

Before PBAs, which evolved over a period of time and which were really perfected in the 1960s, minor-league teams were all independent operations—they functioned on their own as professional baseball teams, getting players where they could, running their own field-management operations, paying their own players. Owners were interested in winning games, improving attendance figures, and selling the contracts of their players to the majors. Of course the big-league teams didn't see the minors this way at all—they thought of them as the training ground for talent for their own teams.

It was Branch Rickey, when he was working for the St. Louis Cardinals before World War II, who first recognized that a farm system run by the major-league team would be the best assurance of a continuing supply of talent. He hired lots of players, assigning them not to the major-league team, but to a series of farm clubs, depending on their skills. In this way, he was able to obtain quality out of quantity. Rickey moved his system to Brooklyn after the war, where one of his farm-team prospects was a brilliant young second baseman named Jackie Robinson.

Naturally, other major-league owners couldn't help but notice the success of Rickey's system, and they began establishing farm systems of their own. Minor-league management didn't like this much—having this kind of relationship with a major-league team reduced their profits because they were unable to sell contracts to the majors, and reduced their independence as on-field managers. Still, the temptations were impossible to resist, and independent teams began to disappear, one after the next.

But trouble was brewing for the major leagues, because with more and more minor-league teams to stock with players, the pool of talent was beginning to dry up. Players who seemed to have any potential at all were offered bonuses—the famous "bonus babies" of the 1950s. Most of these bonus babies were a flop in the majors—it's just impossible, even for baseball professionals, to predict with any accuracy who is going to make it to the bigs. The bonuses got bigger and bigger, the farm teams became more and more expensive, and the big-league teams started closing them down. Minor-league baseball went into a severe decline, with the number of teams, and the percentage of profitable teams, declining rapidly in the late 1950s and 1960s. And the teams that were left were almost all owned by major-league teams—only about 20% of minor-league teams were independent operations by the end of the 1950s.

This put the major leagues firmly in charge. If you wanted to run a minor-league franchise, you had two choices: you operated independently and lost your shirt, or you affiliated with a major-league club which, in exchange for owning the contracts of your players, would subsidize your salary expenses and leave you to run the club as a marketing and sales operation.

By 1961, the system was pretty firmly in place when the minors reached what is really the first Professional Baseball Agreement with the major leagues. The minors would accept limitations on the number of franchises, and agree with the principle that they were there to supply the majors with talent. In exchange, the majors picked up a large portion of the bills. This subordination of the minors to the major-league affiliates characterizes, with few exceptions, the relationship of the minors and majors today.

Part of the reason for this relationship stems from the character of the game. Becoming a major-league baseball player requires time and practice and seasoning. Almost no one can play the game at the highest level straight out of college, as is the case in football, for example. Of the 650 or so men who play major-league baseball today, only four have never played in the minors: Dave Winfield, Jim Abbott, Pete Incaviglia, and John Olerud. While the NFL can use colleges as a place to develop players, professional baseball requires an organized system of training:

The Structure of the Minor Leagues

Even the best players require several years of minor-league experience before they're ready for the bigs. This has always been true: name a great player—Aaron, Ruth, Gehrig, DiMaggio, Musial, Mays—all of them required seasoning in the minors before they came up. Of course there are historical exceptions as well, and even a few who went straight from amateur ball to the pros to the Hall of Fame: Sandy Koufax, Mel Ott, Catfish Hunter, Al Kaline, and Frankie Frisch to name some examples. But if you look over the history of baseball, of the more than 13,000 men who've had any significant career in the majors, maybe three dozen have done it without first putting in their time in the bushes.

Out of this necessity has grown the substantial organization of minor-league baseball. The major-league teams view the system, quite rightly, as their investment in the future, and it is not an act of charity when they pay substantial amounts of money to keep these teams going. The responsibilities of the major-league team to their affiliates in the minors have varied over the years. Today, all of the mutual responsibilities of the parent organization and its minor-league affiliates are outlined in the overall Professional Baseball Agreement and in the individual Player Development Contracts that each minor-league team signs with its parent club.

The Professional Baseball Agreement and the Player Development Contract

These are the agreements that keep minor-league teams supplied with players, and outline the specific responsibilities the parent club and the minor-league affiliate must fulfill. The Professional Baseball Agreement provides that: "This standard Player Development Contract shall be the one and only form of working agreement or contract permitted between Major- and Minor-League Clubs." This is something that baseball is not kidding about: if a minor-league team tries "to alter the contract in any way, or to provide any money, equipment, services or other forms of consideration in excess of the obligations in this standard PDC," the President of the National Association is obliged to fine that team $100,000. The fine for any major-league team that tries to do this is $500,000. In other words, better not to try to bend these rules.

While major-league clubs can no longer abandon a minor-league team in the middle of the season, the PBA gives the major-league team the right to assign the Player Development Contract at will in certain situations. This means that a minor-league team can start out with one parent team, and then, because its parent club wants to rearrange its farm teams, or increase or decrease the number of teams it stocks, end up with its contract assigned to a different team.

The PDC provides that all players are employees of the parent club, as are the instructors, the trainers, the coaches, and the managers. The minor-league team has no right to interfere in any way with these contracts. These players can be transferred, reassigned, moved from one minor-league team to another, or moved up to the majors, and the minor-league team has absolutely nothing to say about it. The parent club, of course, pays for transportation when a player is moved from one club to another. The major-league club has to consult with AAA teams before hiring the manager, but no affiliated minor-league team has any real say in who their manager is going to be.

Schedules of the minor-league teams are also controlled by the Professional Baseball Agreement. Triple-A, Double-A, and A-league teams are limited to 142 games for 1993, 140 games in succeeding seasons. Short-season A teams play 78 games in 1993, the rookie leagues play 60. Doubleheaders are limited to three in a full-season team schedule. The opening and closing dates of the leagues are strictly delineated: no earlier than the first Thursday after the major-league opener, and no games after Labor Day. The Agreement provides time for playoff games as well—usually two weeks after the end of the season. The format of the playoffs is left up to the minor leagues, except for the rookie-advanced leagues where a best-of-three format is prescribed. There are no playoffs in the rookie leagues.

The dubious financial condition of many minor-league teams has become part of the lore of the game, but this is one part of baseball legend the major leagues would just as soon see buried. The majors are determined to insure the continuing financial health of the system that provides them with their future talent, so there are strict rules governing the way teams are financially backed, run, transferred, assigned, bequeathed, and sold.

It is a violation of the Agreement to use the team or its protected territorial rights as security for any indebtedness. No sale, transfer, bequest, or gift can occur without the approval in writing of the president of the NAPBL, who determines whether the transaction constitutes a change in the controlling interest and is therefore subject to the rules outlined in the agreement—whether it is a "regulated transaction." These regulated transactions can include all sorts of things besides the actual sale of the team—sales of equity interest, TV- or radio-rights sales, loan agreements, stadium leases, certain concession contracts, and more.

The major leagues (and the minor leagues, too, for that matter) want to know who is joining the business, so biographical information on all protential owners must be submitted to the president of the NAPBL when a sale is contemplated, including personal financial statements from anyone who will be owning more than 5% of a team. If the potential owner is not an individual but a corporation, the league president's office must see their audited financial statements. Each team must have a single individual who is responsible for all club decisions and who will actively participate in the running of the club and regularly attend minor-league and major-league Association meetings.

Owners must prove that they are financially viable, able to maintain an equity-to-liabilities ratio of 55 to 45. The rules for figuring this ratio are specifically outlined in the Agreement. Conflicts of interest are always on the minds of management: if you are a broadcaster, for example, it may be viewed as a conflict of interest to own a team that will be selling broadcast rights. Establishing a local involvement in the team is essential—this is viewed, correctly in my estimation, as essential to a healthy franchise. Without it, there can rarely be the assurance of fan loyalty, an adequate local playing facility, and long-term local government support. If you're planning to relocate the team when you buy, these intentions have to be stated and described in detail at the outset.

All these rules are designed to protect baseball from losing control of extremely valuable assets, and the agreement provides for continuing monitoring of all teams' finances by the NAPBL and the major-league Commissioner's office. Complete audited statements are due to the Commissioner's office at the end of every playing season. And there are fines that can be imposed for noncompliance—as much as $50,000.

The PBA commits the major leagues to maintaining at least 119 minor-league franchises. These include one Triple-A and one Double-A team for each major-league team (through a PDC or through outright ownership). The agreement also obliges the majors to support at least twenty-six Class-A full-season teams, and gives them the right to increase or reduce the number of rookie-league teams and to relocate them as they deem necessary—that is, the teams in the Arizona, Gulf Coast, Appalachian, and Dominican Summer Leagues.

Besides paying all the salaries of the field personnel, the major-league team pays for uniforms and equipment including, but not limited to, bats and baseballs. The parent club also pays for the trainer and medical supplies.

It used to be that all-night bus trips with a game the next day were among the legendary trials of working in the minors—anyway, I seem to remember something like that from books I've read or movies I've seen. Maybe this was once true, and maybe it never was, but it certainly isn't true today. The PBA describes the standards and requirements for travel and lodging, and they are very specific. Any trip longer than 500 miles by bus requires an off day. If there's a trip longer than 500 miles with no off day scheduled, the team has to fly. All one-day "commuter" road trips are limited to no more than 200 miles round trip. All vehicles used by the minor-league team must be approved by the parent club, and you can't use vans for trips of longer than 75 miles in each direction. You can't schedule an intercity flight after a night game until 9 the next morning. And the major-league club has to approve the hotel the minor-league team uses.

The parent club usually agrees to hold one exhibition game with their Triple-A team—important to the minor-league team, because such a game is usually a sellout—though the parent team also allow themselves a way out by including a clause saying that they can choose to pay the minor-league team a fee rather than play the game. Needless to say, major leaguers do not like playing games, exhibition or otherwise, against their Triple-A team. If they win the game, so what? They're supposed to. And if they lose, they'll never hear the end of it. Most years, the major-league team would rather pay the $5,000 or $10,000 to the minor-league team to avoid this kind of lose-lose situation. The major leagues can arrange to play exhibition games with the Class-AA and A teams, but they rarely do.

Major-league teams are entitled to use minor-league players in promotional publications and for personal appearances, just as they are for their major-league players. The major-league club can tell a farm-team player to show up for a promotional appearance, and he is contractually obligated to do so.

In each Player Development Contract, the salaries of all players are listed—with variations depending on the classification. No minor-league players get paid very much: according to the National Association office, the median for a rookie-league player is $850 a month; a Class-A player makes about $1,000 a month; a Double-A $1,500; and the best-paid players in the minors at the AAA level have a median income of about $5,000 a month. And that's for only six months out of the year. But the classification means everything: even meal-money allowances are lower in the lower classifications!

For the minor-league owners, there's plenty to complain about in the Player Development Contract agreement, but the fact remains that the PDCs are the salvation of the minor leagues. Bob Richmond reminded me that twenty years ago, when he first started working in baseball, there were no PDCs and the minors were in terrible shape. Now almost all minor-league teams have guarantees of working agreements with parent clubs. Besides giving them expenses for all equipment and the salaries of the managers, coaches, and players, the PDCs give minor-league teams the guarantee of not being abandoned by the parent club. It used to be that if a major-league team didn't feel it was in their interest to supply players to a given franchise, they'd just close it down—middle of the season or not. That can't happen anymore. It has been the Class-A and the Class-AA teams that have been helped most by the PDC—the Triple-A teams were always more or less okay even without these agreements.

So the continuing health of the minor leagues depends on this sometimes contentious interdependency with the majors. The majors know they can't get along without the minor leagues, and minor-league operators are equally aware of that they have to rely on the majors' good faith in order to continue their operations. And I suppose as in all interdependent relationships, there will always be some areas of conflict and disagreement. But the essential facts are not in dispute: major-league baseball cannot continue to flourish without a healthy minor-league system; the minors have to be professionally run in order to make money for their owners and supply the parent club with new talent; and the parent clubs have to be considerate of the minor-league operators whose teams embody the future of their organizations.

There are uncertainties ahead. The Commissioner's office, if it isn't a completely dead letter at this point, will nevertheless be radically changed over the next few years. How these changes at the major-league level will affect the minors is hard to know at this point. It's certainly safe to say, however, that the fates of major-league baseball and that of minor-league baseball are thoroughly intertwined.

4

Where to Put Your Money: Finding the Right Team

When I bought the Virginia Generals they were—and I don't think anyone will argue with me about this— the worst team in professional baseball. And I don't mean they were "not so hot" or that they were "kind of crummy." They were truly terrible. They had a one-man grounds "crew," and they hired and fired four men for this position before the 1988 season began. The one they started the season with was the ticket taker's son. This was after the previous crew—the general manager's ex-husband—had been canned. The pitching staff were all independent players— unaffiliated with any major-league team, and for good reason. They were awful. Attendance at the run-down War Memorial Stadium in Hampton, Va., built in 1948, averaged about 200 sullen fans a night. One night only 25 people showed up, so the management

announced each fan's name on the PA system to re-
ward them for their loyalty. Stadium maintenance
consisted of replacing the bleacher boards that people fell through—no point in wasting money replacing all of them. You have to really love baseball to
want to buy a team like this. But I do love baseball,
and I did buy the team. Incredibly, I wasn't the only
one who wanted them.

But how do you know the difference between a
team that's worth putting money in and one that
isn't? There are no sure things in investing, but how
can you narrow the odds a bit?

There are more than 150 communities in the U.S.
that support minor-league franchises. Obviously, not
all locations are equally good. Picking the right location is essential to knowing which team is likely to
thrive, so I'd like to discuss some of the factors that
might go into that decision.

Scott Carter, President of the Double-A Harrisburg
Senators, probably has more insight into picking a
place to play ball than anyone else in the business.
Carter was a commercial banker looking around for
a minor-league team to buy in the mid-1980s when
he heard that Jerry Mileur, the owner of the Nashua,
New Hampshire Double-A franchise was ready to sell.
As it turned out, Carter and his partner didn't come
up with the $750,000 that Mileur wanted for the
team, so Mileur never did sell. But Mileur, who
wanted to go back to his full-time occupation of
teaching political science at the University of Massachusetts, was so impressed with Carter that he hired
him as President of the organization. Carter says
there are two ways to revive a team that's not doing

well: one is to do a repair job on an existing franchise. This is what Craig Stein did with the Reading Phillies, and, according to Carter, Stein did a brilliant job with that franchise. The other method is to pick up and start all over again in a new location. Carter decided on the latter approach.

The team was at that time affiliated with the Pirates. Carter immediately recognized that the hard-working steel-town image of Pittsburgh was all wrong for Nashua, a high-tech exurb of Boston. This was just not a town where a Double-A Pittsburgh affiliate could thrive. So he decided that they had to move. He began by undertaking a demographic study of the Eastern-League territories.

The study showed Carter that he needed a certain kind of fan to keep a minor-league team going: the typical fan is a blue-collar worker with income in the $30,000 range, a stable family, and a car loan on the Chevy. Two towns fit the bill: Springfield, Massachusetts and Harrisburg, Pennsylvania. But there was a big problem with Springfield: they had no stadium, and weren't willing to build one. No stadium, no minor-league ball—especially these days when the major leagues have many strict requirements about the facilities their teams can play in.

Harrisburg is in a region that takes sports seriously. Penn State, the Pirates, the Phillies, the Eagles, the Flyers, even the Baltimore Orioles—all these teams have their rabid fans in Harrisburg. A home-town minor-league baseball team seemed a natural.

So Harrisburg it was. Mayor Stephen Reed was eager to have a team. Like many mayors, Reed saw the team as a way to revive a run-down part of town.

In this case, the area was the island in the Sus-quehanna River that divides the town into two halves. The stadium was built on that island, and baseball became, at least symbolically, the factor that unites the two parts of Harrisburg.

In addition to the stadium, Carter says, there are at least two other essentials in locating a team. First, you need a sympathetic local business community. Minor-league teams can't depend on national adver-tisers for their revenue, so they need the local busi-ness to complete the picture. Moreover, the local businesses are the ones that buy season tickets and sponsor promotional events. Without them, it would be almost impossible to operate successfully. Carter's team, like many others, derives one-third of its revenues from advertising, almost all of it local.

Furthermore, you need a good relationship with the local government, whether it's city, county, or state. For Carter, baseball is an amenity for a city, one the city should be willing to encourage over and above whatever economic advantages a team brings. Carter feels that the way to get along with the local govern-ment is to treat its officials as you would a cus-tomer—with concern for their needs and a willingness to go out of your way to please them.

Carter is not laying down the law in any of this. Every team has to operate in its own way according to its circumstances, and you have to gear your team's marketing to the personality of the community. But it's clear that much of what Carter says can be ap-plied to other teams and other markets.

Miles Wolff, former owner of the Durham Bulls, picked not just one city—he picked six of them when

he decided to start a whole new league. The Northern
League operated in this area for many years, but
Wolff was going back into a territory that now lacked
professional baseball of any kind. This new league
started play in June 1993 with teams in Duluth, St.
Paul, and Rochester, Minnesota; Sioux City, Iowa;
Sioux Falls, South Dakota; and Thunder Bay, On-
tario.

To get in—obviously, it's too late now for anyone to
invest in these clubs—all you needed was a letter of
credit, sufficient capitalization, and a knowledge of
the risks involved. Players—the first thing you might
think of in a league like this that has no major-league
affiliation and therefore no automatic stocking of talent—are, for Wolff, not a problem. There are plenty of
good players the majors overlook, release, or aren't
interested in, for one reason or another. Wolff feels
that a team like the Salt Lake Trappers proves you
can play minor-league baseball without having your
players paid by a major-league team.

Most of the players in the new Northern League will
be paid around $1,000 a month, and the league will
have salary caps to keep it from getting too much
higher than that. The league will use a clock to enforce the twenty-second pitch rule, a baseball rule
which most fans have probably forgotten about, since
it's never enforced elsewhere. The same clock will give
the batter twenty seconds to get back in and ready to
hit. Wolff says this takes twenty to thirty minutes off
every game. For the most part, the league will use the
old Northern League parks still there from the early
seventies when that league closed up shop. Wolff admits that some of these parks don't come up to the

standards set in the Professional Baseball Agreement—but he points out that a lot of the teams that
function under that agreement don't come up to
those standards either.

Wolff picked his area carefully. This was a part of
the country that once supported minor-league ball,
but was closed out of it during one of minor-league
baseball's low points twenty years ago. People in
these parts haven't seen live professional baseball
since then, and Wolff is counting on their being hun-
gry for it now. The cities in the league have the population and the stadium—the two essential
ingredients—to make minor-league ball a success.

Wolff's owners are mostly old baseball hands.
Ricky May, a former minor-league general manager
who was involved in sports marketing for Valvoline,
will take over the Thunder Bay franchise. Cord
Pereira, who is a VP of the Boise Hawks in the Northwest League, will be running the Sioux City team.
Wolff was more interested in finding the right kind of
business management talent to run his teams than
he was interested in finding big financial backing.
From his point of view, there are plenty of sources of
money, but only limited sources of the kind of baseball experience that makes minor-league teams succeed. He concentrated on finding the right owners,
and let the money take care of itself.

Marv Goldklang is another owner in the new
league. Along with Mike Veeck (son of Bill Veeck), and
the actor Bill Murray, he'll be running the St. Paul
Saints, whose 72-game season started June 15,
1993. Goldklang came into baseball in the early
80s—his first team, and my first association with

him, was when he became a part owner of the Utica Blue Sox. Goldklang is a lawyer and an investment banker, and he became interested because one of his law firm's clients was looking for financing for the concessions stands in our park. He wanted to know how much of the team he could have if he financed the stands himself. In those days, that was enough to get you in, so Goldklang became one of our partners. Until that moment, the idea of becoming an owner of a baseball team had never occurred to him.

The Utica Blue Sox were not a great investment—in fact, Goldklang lost whatever he'd put in—a few thousand dollars. But, as he says, he just didn't learn his lesson, and in 1986 he became a minority investor in the Pittsfield Cubs, a Double-A team in the Eastern League. Now he'd had some experience in the operations side of baseball, and he understood that a properly run team could actually make some money. The Pittsfield team was moved to Williamsport, Pennsylvania, where the Mets bought it and moved it to Binghamton, New York in 1989.

In May, 1991, Goldklang bought the Erie Sailors, which he still owns, a team in the Class-A New York-Penn League. The Pennsylvania State Legislature has passed a budget with money for a new stadium for Erie, but Goldklang isn't sure yet if the stadium will actually be built. Erie is a great baseball town, and the team now has a four-year PDC agreement with the Texas Rangers, but the stadium he's playing in is nowhere near what the PBA demands. Among other defects, it has a right-field line that's 280 feet and can't be extended because there's an elementary school right outside the fence. His target gate for getting the new park in Erie is June 1994—if it goes much beyond that, he feels he'll probably have to move the team.

But his chief preoccupation now is the new Northern League. He's looking forward to participating actively in the talent side of the game. As a minor-league owner, Goldklang says, he often feels like a movie-theater operator—he sells the popcorn, but the creative side of the operation is left to someone else—the people who make the films. With the independent St. Paul team, he'll be in the action developing player personnel and making decisions about the team on the field as well as off. He's already had some experience with this, since he also ran the Miami Miracle (now the Fort Myers Miracle) an independent team in the Florida State League. At that time, a provision of the PBA allowed Class-A teams to participate in the professional baseball draft, and the Miracle did so, signing fifteen of the sixteen players they drafted. He enjoyed working with the players immensely, tried hard, often successfully, to make their careers move on and transfer their contracts to major-league clubs, and made many close friends among the players and their families. Goldklang sees the Northern League as an opportunity to continue this kind of work, which he finds immensely rewarding.

There is some chance that the league, which now has six teams, will soon go to eight. There were plenty of people who wanted in to this league—many more than there were actually franchises to buy. But this is a place where a potential investor certainly ought to be looking at this point, and he could start by calling up Miles Wolff, who is the President of the league and its guiding spirit. According to Goldklang, what's needed is a $100,000 letter of credit, plus some baseball expertise. At the end of two years, if you want to stay in the league, you'll have to pay a $50,000 franchise fee. Obviously, there are plenty of people who have this kind of money—the league wants to make sure some knowledge of the baseball business comes with it.

In addition to the salary cap to prevent unrestricted bidding wars among owners, and the twenty-second rule, there will be some other innovations. Each team will have four veteran slots which can be filled by former major leaguers, plus five slots that have to be filled by first-year professionals. The designated-hitter rule will be in effect with a twist: each manager will have two opportunities per game to use a designated hitter instead of his pitcher. After he uses up the two at bats, the pitcher has to hit or come out. This may not seem like a big change, but in a world as tradition bound as baseball, it's pretty radical.

Each club will scout players on their own, but the league will have a director of player development who will also do scouting and tryouts. They'll grade the talent for the league, acting almost as an employee search firm for the teams. The league's objective is to demonstrate that independent baseball can still work, developing players and eventually selling their contracts to major-league clubs. Goldklang is convinced that the level of play will be close to Double-A, and he has reason to be optimistic about fans' reaction to the new teams: he had sold 300 season tickets for the St. Paul Spirits by December of 1992, he has a handsome, recently expanded 5,000-seat stadium to play in, and, like most true baseball fans, he just can't wait till spring.

The Northern League isn't the only new league that will start operating in 1993. It was announced in November, 1992 that a new eight-team Texas-Louisiana League will start operating as a short season A-league. The president of Texas Baseball, Inc., Byron Pierce, a Dallas businessman, says that they'll be trying to line up player development contracts, but even if they don't succeed, they'll be operating as an independent league. Like the Northern League, they won't be part of the National Association. Pierce has stadiums all lined up—and he says they're Double-A quality, meeting all the requirements of the Professional Baseball Agreement.

Richard Holtzman is an owner of four different minor-league teams, so he has had solid experience in deciding where to put money in baseball. He has ownership interest in the Astros' Triple-A Tucson Toros, the Chattanooga Lookouts, who are the Reds' Double-A team, and two Class-A affiliates, the Albany Polecats (Expos) in the Southern League, and the Quad City River Bandits (Angels) in the Midwest League.

In 1986, when he bought his first team, the Midland Angels in the Texas League, he was coming into a decent baseball city, but a very depressed economic scene—the oil and gas depression had hit the Midland-Odessa area extremely hard, and it wasn't easy getting the city to spend money on baseball when it had lots of other problems to deal with. But Holtzman did succeed in convincing the city that they should match the team's expenditures in upgrading the park, and once they did, the team began to thrive even in a city that was going through some hard times. The confidence that he would be able to do this was an essential factor in deciding to put money into the franchise.

In Albany, Georgia, the situation was somewhat different. This was to be the home of an expansion franchise in the Sally League, and here was a city that had already passed a referendum authorizing the building of a new park to attract the team. Holtzman's team had to spend a year in Sumter, South Carolina waiting—he knew at the outset that Sumter was no place to have a profitable team—but he planned at the end of that year, to move to a new stadium and a better baseball town. Even when Albany's mayor was replaced by a new mayor who was much less enthusiastic about baseball, and in fact came out publicly against the new stadium, it was too late to stop the park from being built. As often happens, once the park was built a successful season followed. This made everyone—even the reluctant new mayor—into a baseball fan and a fan of the Polecats.

Holtzman was similarly successful in Davenport, Iowa with the Quad City team. The park that the team was playing in when he bought the team was in sad shape, and he knew he'd need the city's help to make it the kind of place where professional baseball could be played. In 1987, he went to the mayor and laid his cards on the table: if Davenport wanted pro baseball, they'd have to work on the facility. And work they did. Mayor Thomas Hart invested over $5 million of the city's money in a massive renovation of the park— and attendance went from 44,000 the previous year to 260,000 the first year in the new home. From the city's point of view, this was not at all a bad way to spend tax dollars.

Then there are the harder cases. Chattanooga was not at all an easy road for Holtzman, and the improvements to the stadium there were had at the price of an ugly, and personally painful, public debate. After a year of battling, he did succeed in getting the city to put $2.5 million into the stadium, but it wasn't easy, and the battle left a lot of people unhappy, not least of all Holtzman himself. There was even a lawsuit against the city—with a judgment in favor of the team—to get $500,000 to repair the new field, which didn't drain properly. At one point, he had to use the owner's ultimate weapon—the threat to move the team out of the city, which is an atomic bomb of a public statement that's very hard to recover from. Some people buy teams with the intention of moving them immediately, but Holtzman doesn't like to do this. At the same time, he fully realizes that if you make the threat, you have to be prepared to act on it. For Holtzman, this situation represents the downside of the local ownership that the National Association encourages: local owners have less leverage with a city because they can't move the team. Sometimes teams just flounder with local ownership, playing in inadequate facilities in front of small crowds, and losing money year after year because a city doesn't feel obliged to contribute to the maintenance of the park. Sometimes entrenched local ownership creates a situation that a potential investor should be wary of.

Holtzman readily admits that baseball is not the

equivalent, for a city government, of a police and fire department, but (and of course he's not the first to say this) it is an amenity that makes a city a more attractive place to live, and it can and does have significant positive economic impact. Minor-league baseball can't thrive without the cooperation of local governments, and cities that lack amenities like professional baseball remain, in some sense, second class.

PART THREE

The Art of Investing in Minor-League Baseball

5

Investing

The Colorado Rockies and the Florida Marlins, the
two new national-league expansion teams, are in the
process of setting up their own farm systems. They
must have one Triple-A and one Double-A franchise
each, and the competition among cities for these
franchises has been just as intense as the competition for the location of the two parent clubs. These
locations and ownership arrangements were determined by the time of the Winter Meetings in 1992.
The Marlins will have their Triple-A team in Edmon-
ton, and the Rockies will affiliate with the Colorado
Springs team in the Pacific Coast League. Neither
team will have a Double-A affiliate until 1994. Obviously, it's a bit late to get involved in the ownership of
these teams—they've been going through the appli-
cation process for some time, and their backers finalized and known to all.

But both the Rockies and the Marlins will be setting up Class-A teams as well—they've already got one each, plus a rookie-league team, but they'll need more. Here's where the investor has to do some research, and he should begin it by calling the offices of the various A-league presidents. You'll find the names and numbers in an Appendix to this book. There isn't any way to know at this point where these teams will be located, which leagues will want to expand to accommodate the new teams, or whose money will form the initial investments. At this point, both the South Atlantic League and the New York-Penn League have contemplated expansion, but no one yet knows what will happen.

Where the money goes in a minor-league operation

If you're going to invest, you have to know where your money is going to go, so here I'm going to show you a typical team's expenses—how a minor-league team spends money to make the revenues come in from gate receipts, advertising, and concessions. These facts and figures come from the actual expenses of a Double-A team. The expense items I present here and the figures cited are quite typical for this level of minor-league franchise. Let's call the team the Middletown Bulldogs.

The Bulldogs play in the Texas League, a league that requires air travel. This is true of all three Triple-A leagues, and some of the Double-A's as well. There's no way that the Texas League could get away with using buses. The distances are too great. Air travel costs money, and the Bulldogs spend $75,000 a year taking the team to visiting parks. There are eight road trips a year, so each time you go out of town you're spending around $9,500—and you're taking in absolutely nothing, since it's only the home team that collects gate receipts—no sharing allowed.

While you're on the road, you have to have some-where to sleep. The $35,000 the Bulldogs spend on motels is about average for their league. You normally have to put up the umpires when you play at home, but Middletown offered a local motel some free adver-tising in their scorecard in exchange for rooms for the umps, so there was no outlay there. Add in about $3,300 for incidental uniform expenses (the Bulldogs don't buy the uniforms, but they do repair them), and that about covers money spent on the guys who work between the lines. Remember that there are no sala-ries or regular uniform and equipment expenses for players, coaches, or the manager—the major-league affiliate picks up those expenses.

That takes care of the players and the road trips. Now come the big expenses: running the business at home. Naturally, there's a cost to selling tickets. In the first place, you have to print them. The Bulldogs rent computer equipment—CRTs, printers, software, modems, the whole nine yards—from a ticket agency for ten months out of the year, at $440 a month. The team prints season-ticket books, season passes, parking-lot tickets and tags, and box-seat coupons. They pay a ticket manager, and during the season they hire additional people to sell tickets. Even though these are usually minimum-wage employees, it starts to add up.

The Bulldogs run an aggressive campaign before the season starts to sell season tickets by telephone. These "book sales" start with some ads in the paper to hire people to do the telemarketing. Then they install a bunch of extra phone lines for the three-month sales period. There's a director of telephone sales who does the hiring and runs the operation. He gets a salary. The telephone salespeople earn commissions on their sales, plus a (very modest) salary. The team does mailings to likely customers, nice looking four-color brochures that, along with postage, cost more than $5,000 to put into people's hands. Season tickets and tickets to big advertisers are often delivered by hand, so about $1,300 is paid for messengers every year. By the time they're done selling season tickets, usually by the end of March, they've spent nearly $22,000.

The Bulldogs have a "President's Club" for season-ticket holders and big advertisers. These are special customers who get special treatment—dinners, various jackets, caps, bats, and baseballs, and a trip to California to see a major-league team play at the end of the season. These people pay for the privilege, of course, and the Bulldogs make money on the deal, but there are expenses, as well: about $15,000.

When a corporation buys a large number of tickets for a single game to take their employees out to the ballpark, the Bulldogs print special tickets with the corporation's name on them. There are about fifteen of these "buyouts" a year, averaging about $500 in extra costs per night.

Printing is a large expense for any club—not just tickets, but programs, scorecards (which of course have to be changed regularly for each visiting team), a four-color yearbook, roster sheets, business cards, menus for the restaurant in the stadium and for the skyboxes, letterhead and envelopes, promotional calendars, contest inserts, a newsletter, advertising brochures, and rate cards—there's a blizzard of paper going out of the club's offices every year, and all of it has to be designed, proofed, typeset, and printed to look right. Even though Middletown managed to save some money this year by finding a college kid who knows desktop publishing and has a good eye for design, they're still spending about $40,000 to get all this material together.

Then there are the routine office operational expenses—everything from hiring Roto-Rooter to get the infield dirt out of the plumbing system to buying pom-poms for the ballgirls to paying the Red Cross for first-aid supplies and a cot. This costs about $30,000 a year. Business travel to Double-A meetings, Texas League meetings, the big Winter Baseball Meetings, and a couple of other affairs costs $6,000 a year.

The stadium has a lease—the team pays the City of Middletown $5,000 a year, and then spends additional money maintaining the scoreboard, the electrical system, the security alarms, and the office equipment. They also pay a statistics service to collect and compute the numbers on their players. This year the sound system kept acting up, and they had to spend $1,200 getting the electricians to fiddle with it. These lease and maintenance contracts add up to around $15,000. The Bulldogs have a parking lot that they maintain (and of course collect parking fees on). That costs about $1,500 a season. The team subscribes to *Baseball America* (the minor-league's trade paper) and to the *Sporting News* and the *Official Airlines Guide.* That's about $200 for magazines.

Bathroom supplies cost plenty. Don't forget: this isn't an ordinary office with a few toilets and sinks. There are locker rooms—two of them—filled with whirlpools and such things, and there are laundry bills for dirty uniforms that you have to see to believe. Just keeping clean costs the team $12,000 a season.

Stadiums have lights, big ones, and the electric company won't let you turn them on unless you pay the bill: the Bulldogs spend $313 dollars for electricity every home game, plus another hundred bucks to light up their scoreboard. That's *per game,* and the team plays seventy home games a year plus exhibitions. They have some outside lighting, too, including an electric marquee that runs all year round and costs $11,000 a year to power. The food in the concession stands is cooked and kept warm with gas, so the gas company gets theirs as well. All told, the team had about $60,000 in electric and gas bills last year.

Lawyers. Oh, yes. And accountants. Any business needs them, and they cost the Bulldogs about $15,000 a year. Then there's insurance, which is one of the biggest expenses for a minor-league team. Like any other business, the team has to spend plenty on health insurance (their biggest insurance expense by far), workmen's compensation, liability, and fire and theft policies. They also have policies on the partners. But a baseball team has some special kinds of insurance that few other businesses would need. For example, the Bulldogs have rain insurance. Fifteen dates a year, usually the big promotional nights, are covered. Baseball is a business in which a few rainy days can cause red ink at the end of the season, and it's an article of faith among minor-league operators that it's better to have good weather than a good team. So Middletown not only talks about the weather, but also actually does something about it. For $12,000, an insurance company guarantees clear skies for those big nights. They also insure some of their promotions. For example, the team has a promotion in which they promise to give $1 million to a lucky ticket holder if, say, the fourth batter in the fifth inning hits a grand slam. Not very likely to happen, of course, but this is baseball, and you never know. Just in case, the conservative folks who run the Bulldogs buy a policy: $2,000 guarantees that someone else will pay the $1 million if the improbable occurs. Total insurance bill for the club: $90,000 a year.

Maintaining a professional playing field, particularly under the new standards promulgated by the major leagues, is expensive. It requires lots of equipment, and some people w   know how to use it. You'd think that with dirt all over the place, you wouldn't have to go out and buy the stuff, but a professional infield requires just the right kind of dirt: $7,000 worth, in the case of Middletown. You want grass? $3,500 for fertilizer and chemicals, and another $3,000 for seed. $850 to maintain the lawn equipment. You need a chalker to make the lines, and you need mats, tools, sandbags, aerators, and bases and plates, which wear out faster than you'd think: $3,500. Add in paint, gas, irrigation equipment, and other miscellaneous items, and maintaining the field costs the Bulldogs more than $26,000 a year.

With major-league teams, a radio or TV station will pay to broadcast the games. Not so for the vast major- ity of minor-league teams. The minors view game broadcasts (and they're usually radio only) as three- hour advertisements for the team, and they often pay the radio station to do the broadcasting. They also pay the salaries of the announcer, plus meal money and motel allowances for him when the team is on the road. The team has a flagship station hooked up by telephone to other local stations, and they pay $5,000 a year for long-distance charges for the broad- casts. In total, the radio broadcasts of the team's games cost the Bulldogs a little more than $30,000 a year.

The team also buys other advertising. Middletown pays for a good portion of it—almost half—by trading advertising with the radio and TV stations. They fig- ure that they trade about $60,000 worth of advertis- ing, and then pay another $76,000 in cash for the rest, most of it on TV and radio. They spend only about $5,000 on print advertising in local newspa- pers. Add in about $20,000 for three billboards that they post around town, and you have a total advertis- ing budget of about $104,000.

Like all minor-league teams, the Bulldogs run a promotion of some kind almost every night (see Chapter 6 for the kinds of things minor-league teams get involved in) and most of it is paid for by the adver- tiser. If Planter's Peanuts wants to give away baseballs with their logo on them, the firm usually pays the cost of buying those balls. But a certain percentage is picked up by the team. Of the $213,000 spent on in-stadium promotions, the Bulldogs pay $62,000, or about 30% of the bill.

The team pays about $92,000 a year in taxes on tickets, souvenirs, programs, food, franchise, parking, property, and employment. And the major leagues impose a tax as well: 5% of the team's gate receipts—approximately $42,000. Finally, there's debt service of about $115,000 a year, and League and National Association dues, which add up to $24,300 a year for a team like Middletown. Add in $5,000 in public relations (client lunches, etc.) and about $5,000 in charitable contributions.

All this makes a grand total for the operation of a successful Double-A league team about $1,750,000 a year in expenses. The revenue side is a much simpler affair. For any team, there are only three sources of money, and for a team like the fictional Middletown Bulldogs, you would expect a breakdown something like this:

Ticket sales: $967,123
Concession sales (including parking fees):
$350,000
Advertising revenue: $520,000

That's a total of nearly $2,100,000 in revenue, for a profit of $87,123 at the end of the year. Of course, there's plenty of variation among different teams, even teams in the same league, both on the expense side and the revenue side. I've chosen to invent here a team that's spending carefully, promoting and selling their product efficiently, and making good money. It may be that Middletown is a good baseball market, that the city has just built the team a new stadium, that a new owner has come in and shaken the place up. Reasons for success are as varied as reasons for failure. But any expert looking at a description like this would agree that it presents a pretty fair picture of the operations of a minor-league team.

Just to make sure that the picture I drew here wasn't too far off the mark, I checked with just such an expert: Steve Resnick, C.P.A., of Resnick, Amsterdam, and Leshner, a firm that probably consults financially with more minor-league teams than any other single firm in the country. The firm does general accounting for all kinds of businesses, but Resnick himself specializes in minor-league baseball. He got his first look at these operations from a financial point of view when Craig Stein had him working on the Reading Phillies' books in the mid-1980s. Later, he became an owner himself when he teamed up with Stein to buy the Memphis Chicks. Resnick is no longer an owner, but he's still the accountant for several different teams, and he handles several major-league players' tax planning and preparation as well. (It's not easy being a major-league taxpayer—depending on the league you're in, you work in at least a dozen or more different states that require you to file tax forms—not to mention the city forms and the Canadian forms that all major leaguers have to file. But that's another story.) Resnick has developed a national reputation for his baseball work.

Resnick, who has been a baseball fan all his life, now finds himself seeing forty or fifty games a year all over the country, so he's seen all sorts of teams with all sorts of ownership philosophies. Resnick says a well-run team usually has 20% to 25% of its income already in the bag on opening day from advance advertising revenue and season-ticket sales. From there, teams have variable income—some extra advertising here and there, the daily gate receipts, and the "per caps" as they are known in the industry—the extra money that each fan spends in addition to the price he paid for the ticket. This is the money a team has to work hard for all year long—and they have to be lucky, too. Having a winning team may not be so important as it is in the majors—fans come to see minor-league teams for other reasons—but things like weather reports take on life-or-death meaning as the season wears on. One big promotion rained out can spell big trouble for any team, particularly those at the lower levels.

I asked Resnick about the small investor—the guy with $2,000 who'd like to put it in a minor-league team. He says there are few places to do that anymore. It used to be a lot easier when the perceived value of the teams was much lower (and matched by much lower operating revenues than are typical today), but these are different times.

The great majority of investment opportunities in minor-league ball are restricted to those who have more than $25,000 to put in. Ten or fifteen years ago, this wasn't the case, but times have changed. Today, the National Association discourages breaking up a team into many little parts, and this has left the person with $1,500 or $2,000—which not long ago was enough money to buy an entire franchise—out in the cold. You have to hunt for places where you can still put this kind of money into a team, have some fun doing it, expect any decent return on your money, and have a feeling that your participating in any significant way.

Because of these facts of life in the minors, the day of the sole operator has pretty much passed. Once an energetic person could get a stake together, buy a team, and make it work. Now, so much money is required to get started that it isn't realistic to expect one person to come up with the money—even if there are people who have the money to spend, the risks are greater, and hardly anyone would want to take them on alone.

But there is one operator among the 150-plus teams out there who still goes it alone, and it's worth taking a look at the way he does it, in part to see how it used to work in the old days, and in part to see how an unusual person might still be able to make it work today. His name is Dennis Bastien, and he owns and operates the Charleston Wheelers, a Class-A team in the Sally League.

Bastien's first job in baseball began in 1979 with the South Atlantic League team in Gastonia, North Carolina. He did such a good job in reviving this dying franchise (becoming minor-league Executive of the Year in the process) that the league asked him to go to Macon, Georgia to, as Bastien puts it, "give mouth-to-mouth resuscitation to a dead-horse franchise."

The Macon team in 1982 was nothing if not a dead horse. When he arrived, he found that the IRS had padlocked the park because they believed, correctly as it turned out, that the team owed them $85,000. Seems the owners had had the parent club do the payroll, which they then passed on to the players. But they neglected to give the government their share of the withholding. The tax people, naturally, took a dim view of this, so before he could even get into the place, he had to raise $85,000 from local people to pay off the IRS. The league wanted Bastien to buy the team—but he resisted buying an organization where some creditor he'd never heard of was always knocking on the door asking to be paid. No one even knew where the next bill was coming from, much less how much the bill was going to be.

Then he set to work all by himself—painting signs, selling advertising, doing door-to-door ticket sales, designing and carrying out promotions. He worked, as is his custom, about twenty hours a day at it. In the end, it paid off—the team made about $15,000 the first year—which would have been over $100,000 without the debts that the absentee owners had left him. Needless to say, when they noticed that the team had miraculously revived itself, they showed up, decided they could do it themselves now that Bastien had showed them how, and they fired him.

Spartanburg in 1983 was Bastien's next stop. The situation here was almost, but not quite, as bad as the one in Macon. Again, Bastien managed almost single-handedly to put the team into the black essentially by doing everything himself, including construction work wherever the old park needed it. It was in that summer of 1983 that he got a bit tired of doing it for other people, and decided that it was about time to be an owner himself. He persuaded his father to take out a mortgage on the family farm, and he used the money—discovering the true meaning of the word "stress" in the process—to buy the moribund Winston-Salem franchise in the Carolina League.

As a ball team, Winston-Salem had done pretty well the previous year—in fact, they had the best won-lost record in the minors. But as a business operation, they were truly terrible. Despite the winning season, they'd drawn only 50,000 fans. The previous owner did nothing with the team all winter long—he'd open up the stadium in March and hope for the best. This was the kind of situation that Bastien knew something about, and he set to work in the fall of 1983 to make the Winston-Salem Spirits (one of his first moves was to give the team this new name) into a profitable baseball operation.

When he arrived, there was no office in the stadium, so he built one. By himself. He moved into the locker room, since he had no place else to stay, and lived there until the season opened. And he began to work his marketing and sales magic once again. On February 1, he got married, and his wife Lisa went to work for the team too. He moved out of the locker room just in time for the beginning of the season—one in which the team was terrible, but the attendance nearly doubled to 95,000. And the team started to make money.

In 1987, looking for a slightly bigger market with correspondingly bigger challenges, Bastien sold the Winston-Salem team and bought the Charleston

Wheelers in the South Atlantic League. He and Lisa moved to West Virginia, and have been running this Cincinnati Reds A-level team ever since.

Dennis Bastien has never had a job outside of baseball, which also makes him rather unusual as an owner these days. At one time, no one except career baseball people were interested in owning minor-league teams. Now hardly any career baseball people own them. Bastien may be the last of a peculiar breed: the minor-league owner who owns 100% of the team, lives in the town, sells advertising, sweeps the dugouts, pulls the tarp, checks the hot-dog supply, and pays attention to every other little detail that makes the difference between a profitable team and a loser. He doesn't consult with a Board of Directors in Los Angeles when there's a decision to be made: he makes it himself, and he and his community live with it. He still thinks this is a better situation to be in for a minor-league owner, and I'll bet that a lot of his colleagues would agree with him, even though they can't emulate him.

Money: Getting and Spending

If you ask minor-league owners—the successful ones—how to make money in baseball, they'll answer, almost unanimously, that the only way to assure success is to get people to pay their way into games. Both Miles Wolff and Bob Richmond say that owners are making a big mistake if they give away tickets to a game and hope to make a profit selling hot dogs. This is not to say that concessions aren't important—as we'll see later in this chapter, they're essential to the success of a ball club. But the only solid basis for an ongoing business is the number of fans who come to the park. The other sources of income—parking fees, concessions, and advertising—all depend on filling the seats with paying customers.

Some owners are tempted to give away tickets in large numbers to get more people in, brag about the high attendance figures they get when they add in all the freebies, sell more advertising on that basis, and cover their costs by making money on concessions. This is a big mistake. When you give something away for nothing, people conclude that that's about what it's worth. The whole idea of giving away tickets is self-defeating. Bob Richmond, who has looked into this carefully, has numbers that prove that people who get in for free actually spend less on food and souvenirs than people who pay their way in. Whatever justification there was for giving away the tickets obviously disappears in the face of statistics like that.

Jack Cavanaugh, writing in the *New York Times* last year, described a family going to a New Britain Red Sox game—the Britsox are a Red Sox Double-A affiliate in the Eastern League. The group—a father, his five kids, and two of their friends—spent $14 on tickets, or roughly the same price as one ticket to see the Red Sox at Fenway. Joe Buzas, the owner of the team, feels that in recessionary times, prices like these are helping the minor-leagues thrive.

Dealing with local governments

If you're going to be a baseball owner, you're going to have to learn to understand politics and get along with politicians. There's no way for a baseball team to proceed without the help of government, and no matter how independent-minded an owner may be, he's going to have to get used to this idea or get out of the game.

When Eric Margenau and I bought the South Bend

White Sox, part of the reason the team was available was that the previous owners were exhausted from the legal battles that went on before the stadium was built. The South Bend White Sox are the first full-time professional team ever to play in South Bend, but putting them there was quite a chore.

South Bend is a blue-collar town of about 100,000 people. When the Studebaker plant there closed down in 1964, it was the beginning of an economic decline for the city that persists today. Roger Parent, who became mayor in 1984, was determined to turn the city around, and one of the ways he wanted to do it was to build a stadium and put pro baseball in South Bend. When the Class-A Midwest League proposed a team for South Bend, Parent wanted to hear more. Concentrating on downtown redevelopment, Parent wanted to make the stadium an important part of this urban-renewal project, and of course the White Sox wouldn't put a team there without a professional-level stadium to play in.

It's kind of odd that a man like Parent became the champion of baseball in South Bend. He's not even really a baseball fan, much less an athlete himself. He has more of an academic bent than most politicians, and he's about as different from the people you usually see in the baseball business as night from day. But he was determined to see baseball come to South Bend not because he wanted to sit in a skybox and watch games, but because he profoundly believed that it was the route to urban redevelopment in a part of the city that really needed it.

Rich Hill was the city attorney at the time, and it was part of his job to help find the financing to make the project work. He recalls that Parent initially tried to have the state impose a food and beverage tax to raise the money for the stadium, a proposal that was met with absolutely no support whatsoever in the state legislature. When that failed, Parent tried to gather signatures for a general obligation bond—but that failed, too, because in Indiana you can defeat such a proposal by gathering even more signatures against it, which is exactly what the citizens of South Bend did. Finally, the mayor was able to get the city council to agree to pass a lease-purchase arrangement. By this technique, a bank in California—Security Pacific—would pay for the stadium and own it, and then lease it back to the city, in effect having the bank act as the bondholder. The State was willing to go along with this, and after this long fight, the financing for the stadium was in hand.

But that wasn't the end of it. Just as the ink was drying on the financing agreements, the people who owned the franchise—a young couple named Staley and a man called John Wendel—ran out of patience. It was clear to Hill that they were planning to sell. They'd bought the franchise for $20,000, so when we offered them $455,000 for it, they were happy to get out of baseball in South Bend—and out of politics.

By this time, the stadium was half finished, and we knew we had to get that park built and negotiate a lease to use it if South Bend was going to have a team—and if our investment was going to pay off. You have to understand that Roger Parent was acting without much in the way of public support for his point of view, but, according to Rich Hill, he felt that it was his job to lead in this instance and not to follow. It also has to be said that Parent was in a position to act decisively and on his own instincts: he had already decided not to run for a third term as mayor. Some said that the stadium cost him a third term, but in fact he never planned to run in any case.

In Hill's view, and in mine, Parent turned out to be right. The stadium, and the South Bend White Sox, have been a tremendous success for the city. The area around the stadium has been redeveloped. The city has begun to clean up the vast, largely abandoned, Studebaker property that abuts the new field. The whole neighborhood looks better, and the team has been embraced by the community—not least by some of those who were the most vociferous in opposing the construction of the stadium.

But when Eric Margenau and I came into the picture after buying the team from the original owners, Parent was—and this was kind of puzzling to me—playing hardball. At first, he just refused to talk to us. He threatened that he didn't have to talk to us, or to anyone else for that matter, and that if all they played in his new park was American Legion ball, that was okay with him. He did, of course, eventually start to talk to us, thanks in large part to the efforts of Rich Hill.

When we came into the deal, we thought the lease was pretty much worked out—but almost nine months of tough bargaining followed. I'm not complaining—Hill and Parent fought a good fight, and got a good deal for the city of South Bend. And I think in the end, Margenau and I got a good deal too. We operated the team, made money doing so, and sold the team at a large profit at the end of a couple of years.

And the new stadium and the new team have done South Bend a world of good economically. The current mayor, Joe Kernan, a former Notre Dame baseball star who was the controller during the Parent administration, is a frequent attendee at the park, and even many of the people who opposed building the stadium are now great supporters of the team.

Politicians come and go, and sometimes a mayor who's a baseball fan is replaced by one who is not. That happened in Albany, Georgia when Richard Holtzman, the owner of the Albany Polecats, set about getting a stadium built in that town. The city wanted to build the park, and passed a referendum to do just that. But Tom Coleman, the mayor and baseball fan, was replaced by a new mayor who was at best indifferent to the project. He said publicly that he was not in favor of it, but it was too far along for him to actually stop it. Let's just say that his enthusiasm for it was well under control as the project went haltingly forward. When the stadium was finished, though, and as it filled up with happy fans, the mayor, too, became a baseball fan—just as in South Bend, once the park was built, even those who opposed it came around.

Often, it is the additional uses to which a stadium can be put that swings the deal for a city. When Frank Boulton structured his agreement so that Wilmington would get a community facility out of the deal, spending the $5 million of taxpayers' money to put it up looked a lot more possible. If that deal works the way Boulton wants it to, the city of Wilmington will be getting a stadium that they won't have to spend any money maintaining.

Delaware appropriated $4 million for the stadium,

and the state put some conditions on the grant: the money could not be spent until a minor-league team agreed to occupy the stadium; the stadium had to be available for community use; and the owner of the team had to have a financial stake in the stadium to prevent him from packing up and moving as soon as some other city offered him a deal. In the end, the state government came up with $4 million, the city of Wilmington added $2 million, and private investors supplied the rest. South Bend went about it a little more loosely—they didn't have a commitment from a team when the stadium started to go up, which put them in a much weaker negotiating position by the time a team was ready to talk. But in every case, the baseball team holds a strong position: the National Association divides the country into territories, only one team can negotiate for a given location. The city or state government either talks to that team or to none.

Professional baseball is perfectly aware of the value of this system of dividing the country into territories, and minor league territorial rights are outlined very carefully in the Professional Baseball Agreement (see Chapter 3 for a more detailed description of this document). The Agreement grants "protected territory" to each minor-league team.

Cities are eager to have baseball—there is no doubt about this. In the late 1980s, Raleigh, North Carolina became very jealous of nearby Durham which was getting lots of attention for, and considerable economic benefit from, the Durham Bulls. There was some talk of moving the Bulls to Raleigh—they play in a very modest park in downtown Durham and were in a position to be lured away—but when that failed, Raleigh put out an official "Request for Proposal" for fielding a professional baseball team. Even though they knew that they were proposing a team within the Bulls' 35-mile limit that the National Association enforces, they specified in the "Request for Proposal" that this obstacle would have to be overcome by getting an exception to the rule. Raleigh advertised itself in the "Request" as enjoying "a very hospitable climate with mild winters and perfect baseball springs and summers," and bragged of its four TV stations, its many radio stations, its two daily newspapers, its fifty hotels, and its well-funded Convention and Visitors' Bureau. But probably the most important part of the "Request"—the first place a baseball owner who saw some potential in the city would look—was one sentence that read: "Raleigh is actively interested in once again hosting a professional baseball team and to promote the acquisition of a team, the City intends to build, in conjunction with North Carolina State University, a 6,000-seat baseball stadium, funds for which were approved by the voters of Raleigh in October, 1987." Although Raleigh never did get a team, this is the music a minor-league owner wants to hear a city playing.

Stadium facilities

Cities and baseball teams are married to each other for better or worse. It is a relationship fraught with the problems that any interdependency can lead to, and the center of all conflict is almost always the construction and maintenance of the stadium.

The biggest problem a team faces is finding the right place to play. There was a time when a minor-league team could play just about anywhere there was a home plate, three bases, and some grass—there weren't any requirements to be met. But now the major leagues require that their affiliates play on fields, and in stadiums, that are up to specific standards, all carefully outlined in the Professional Baseball Agreement.

A Class-A team has to have a seating capacity of at least 4,000, with the numbers going up to 6,000 for AA and 10,000 for a Triple-A team. Short-season A leagues and rookie leagues need 2,500 seats in their parks. And you can't just throw up some bleachers, either. The seats—at least 10% of them—have to be box seats (separate seats with a back) or reserved seats (a bench with a back). The stadium has to have "an accoustically balanced sound system"—not some guy shouting through a megaphone—and the stadium has to be equipped with a scoreboard that provides, at a minimum, line score, ball-strike-out, and the number of the player at bat.

The stadium has to have a visible clock, radio and TV booths that provide a clear view of the field, and a separate area for print media with proper telephone, power, lighting, and furniture fixtures.

The field has to comply with the minimum dimensions specified in the Official Baseball Rules—check sections 1.04 through 1.08 of those rules in case you've forgotten how far it is between bases. The maximum allowable grade from the base of the pitcher's mound to the warning track behind the plate is 6 inches, and the maximum grade from second base to the outfield warning track is 20 inches. In other words, if you play in the minors you play on a (more or less) level playing field. The warning track has to be made out of material that differentiates its feel from the field, and it has to be at least 15 feet wide all the way around. In new facilities, the outfield wall must be permanent, and at least 8 feet high. Foul poles have to be 30 feet high, you must have standardized dugouts, bullpens, a batting cage, and a flagpole. The stadium has to have a "batter's eye"—a mono-chromatic background in the outfield, and even its dimensions are prescribed: a minimum of 16 feet high by 40 feet wide, with a recommendation for new facilities of 40 feet high by 80 feet wide. You need lighting—and it has to be of a specific minimum can-dle power.

All this stuff has to be maintained, and the Profes-sional Baseball Agreement outlines what constitutes acceptable maintenance. As far as the field is con-cerned, the document says that "every reasonable effort shall be made to insure the safety of the players and the smooth play of the game." The turf must be properly maintained—and don't forget the tarps for the infield, pitcher's mound, and batter's box. In case it rains, you'll need drainage—section 13.2.5 will ex-plain it all to you.

The home clubhouse has to be a minimum of 1,000 square feet (750 square feet for the visitors) and have at least 8 showerheads, 2 toilets, 2 urinals, and 4 sinks. You need at least 5 more lockers than there are players on your team, and you need a minimum of 4 more for the coaches. The field manager gets an office, too. It has a separate shower, toilet, and dressing area, along with a desk and a meeting space for 8 to 10 people.

There has to be a properly equipped training room, with a scale, an ice machine, whirlpool baths, treatment tables—and don't forget the stationary bicycle and the weights. You have to have commercial-quality laundry facilities with washers and dryers sufficient for the needs of your players and staff (though you don't have to have a separate room for this—you can keep the laundry equipment in the training room).

The visiting team's clubhouse doesn't need the laundry equipment, but you still have to be a good host—and the PBA tells you exactly how good you have to be: 6 showerheads, 2 toilets, 2 urinals, 4 sinks, a training table, a whirlpool—and a training area of at least 150 square feet in addition to the 750 square feet of locker room space.

You'll need umpires—there's no game without them—and you'll also have to have a private dressing room, shower room, and toilet facilities, with enough lockers to accommodate the number of umpires typically assigned to your level of play.

The public areas of the stadium must have the right kind of plumbing, too: 1 toilet for every 450 men, 1 toilet for every 125 women, 1 urinal for every 125 men.

There must be sufficient parking within a half mile of the stadium: 1 space for every 3 seats. The concession stands have to have 5 linear feet of counter space and one vendor for every 350 seats. You have to have sufficient storage space for concessions—the agreement recommends enough space to store material for the number of games in an average home stand. You must have 1 ticket window and 1 turnstile for every 1,500 seats. You must have a "command post" for your security forces, with provisions for removing unruly patrons, and a first-aid station, preferably manned by certified medical personnel.

And finally, just to make sure you've done everything right, the major-league's Commissioner's office designates inspectors to come out and look over your work. In 1991, they sent people to check out War Memorial Stadium in Hampton, Virginia, where the Peninsula Pilots played at the time. The inspectors found more than fifty different things to complain about, from the lack of a clock on the scoreboard to the condition of the visitors' showers to the size of the dugouts. I've got no complaint with this—War Memorial Stadium just wasn't up to standards, and the major leagues were only confirming what we all knew.

These requirements obviously make for a better experience for the fans, therefore few owners object to them in principle. But they're expensive, and few minor-league teams can meet these kinds of requirements without getting help from local and/or state governments. Every team makes its own deal with the local government, and these can vary widely. Frank Boulton, in his deal with Wilmington, is paying for most of the furnishings of the stadium (though not for the foul poles or the 8-foot wall). The plumbing, the locker rooms, the concession stands and the cooking and storage equipment—all that will be Boulton's expense, and it all has to be up to standard.

Money: Getting and Spending

Cities know that baseball teams generate money. The better the stadium, the more fans show up—and the more money they generate. When the Scranton/Wilkes-Barre Red Barons, the Phillies Triple-A franchise, moved into the new Lackawanna County Multi-Purpose Stadium, it was, according to Pat McKenna, the editor of the Scranton *Times–Tribune,* "definitely a morale builder for an area that has been through some tough economic times lately." The stadium is a $22 million facility—a lot of money, and $13 million of it is county debt. Notice that they've put "multi-purpose" in the name precisely because they want to emphasize that the stadium is not just for baseball—even though everyone knows that the place never would have been built without the presence of the Red Barons. While the Red Barons are the main beneficiary—there's no way to hide this—still, according to the Economic Development Council of Northeastern Pennsylvania, the team generates $7 for every $1 spent at Lackawanna Stadium. Minor-league teams won't play in inadequate stadiums anymore, and if a city is going to keep a team, they have to be ready to help build a home for them—or else the team may pick up and leave, and teams do it every year. If one city doesn't want them, there is a wide choice of cities that do. The Williamsport Mets, a Double-A franchise in the Eastern League, were unhappy with Bowman Field—the second oldest park in the minors. When Williamsport balked at building a new park, the owners—Sterling Doubleday Enterprises, the same people who own the parent club—picked up and moved to Binghamton, New York, where Binghamton Municipal stadium with its 6,000-person capacity was awaiting them. No hard feelings, of course, and not much sentimentality about the hometown, either.

It seems to me perfectly normal for a citizen to wonder why a city should build a stadium so that some private entrepreneurs can make money with it. But as Rich Hill points out, you have to get past the idea that any government project that involves some private person making money is necessarily bad. In fact, Hill feels, and I agree, that cities should be leveraging private investment with public funds. When it's done right, this benefits everyone.

Gate receipts

This is where most of a team's income comes from. You'll hear a lot of stories about how teams make most of their money from selling hot dogs, but it's not so—at least not among the owners who know what they're doing. When you make money selling souvenirs, or hot dogs and beer, you're only keeping around 50% of the gross receipts—less if you have to subcontract the work to a concessionaire. With gate receipts, you keep everything. This is one reason you shouldn't give away tickets. The other is that it cheapens the whole enterprise. You don't have to be a marketing genius to figure out that telling people your product is worth nothing is not a real good idea—pretty soon, they'll start to believe it. Miles Wolff tells me the Durham Bulls never gave away tickets in the entire time he owned the club. Even with the tremendous expansion in the sales of souvenirs that the Bulls have seen in the last few years, it's still the gate that keeps the team in the black. The South Bend White Sox, when I owned them, were taking in $300,000 a year in gate receipts. The Peninsula Pilots take in roughly $50,000. I don't have access to the exact numbers for other teams, but I can estimate with some degree of accuracy that, for example, the Salt Lake City Trappers take in over $600,000 a year in gate receipts, the Durham Bulls make something a little under $1 million, and the Buffalo Bisons, probably the biggest money-maker among minor-league teams, put around $4 million dollars in the bank every year from what comes in at the turnstile.

Promotions

John Thorn, in his marvelous *Whole Baseball Almanac*, recounts a conversation with Dennis Bastien, president of the South Atlantic League's Charleston Wheelers. Seems the Wheelers were rained out several nights in a row, so Bastien came up with the idea to have something called "Noah Night." "Anybody who came dressed as any kind of ark animal and came two by two, we let in free. Anyone who came dressed as Noah, we let in free. And everyone who brought a toy boat, we let in for $1. We had a couple of hundred crazies come in with horns on. One guy wore a rhinoceros nose. Some came with antlers they got off their father's gun rack. And of course, it rained. In the fourth inning, it rained."

Most teams don't demonstrate this kind of imagination, and not all owners have Bastien's good humor, but there is at least one thing that all owners agree on: in the minor leagues, to a much greater extent than in the bigs, you have to have special promotions if you want to put people in the seats. Bob Richmond says that you have to have something going on every night besides baseball—and if you've ever been to a minor-league game, you know what he means. Some people are watching the game; some are talking; some are drinking; some are there to watch the fireworks and the team mascot. It's a social occasion as much as a sporting event, a family-oriented bit of show biz as much as a ballgame. People come out not just because there's a game, but because there's something going on—a show, a giveaway, a special event of one kind or another. The necessity to provide a show has been the mother of all sorts of inventions, some of them completely lunatic.

Rick Wolff, who today is a New York book editor, played a couple of years of minor-league ball in the 1970s. He recalls a general manager named Fritz Colsthen who even managed to find a use for all the broken bats the team had accumulated during a season—nothing must go to waste on a tightly run minor-league club. He invented "Broken Bat Night," a great promotion for the last night of the season in which every kid under 14 gets a genuine minor-league bat, busted by a genuine minor leaguer. Wolff suggested that maybe they ought to have "Free Tape and Nails Night" so the kids could repair all those broken bats, but, even though such a thing is certainly not beyond possibility, there is no record of it actually having happened. But broken bats have been established as a regular, and very popular, minor-league promotion—some teams even manage to sell some of them at the concession stands.

Not all promotions work out as planned. Craig Stein, the imaginative owner of the Double-A Reading Phillies got the idea to retire Mike Schmidt's number—Schmidt had spent time in Reading in his minor-league days, and an appearance by him would certainly draw the crowds—as it probably would in a lot of places. In any case, Stein invited Pete Rose, Schmidt's good friend, to attend the festivities with him. Of course, Rose was supposed to stay away from baseball, and when he turned up on the field to honor his friend, some people in the Commissioner's office got a little upset, to say the least. Stein wasn't looking for this kind of trouble—he was only trying to promote his team—and he found the whole episode pretty uncomfortable. Looking back on it now, it seems to have been much ado about nothing, but at the time, Stein recalls, it was pretty unpleasant.

According to Keith Lupton, general manager of the AA-league Bowie, Maryland team, fireworks is the best promotion of all. A display that costs $3,000 guarantees a full house, and you can usually get someone to sponsor it. Even when there's rain, 4,500 people will show up, and if the weather's good for one of these promotions, Lupton can put as many as 9,000 people in the seats. In addition, the fireworks display is an easy sell to a sponsor. In El Paso, the Diablos have no fewer than ten fireworks nights a season, and all of them bring in the fans.

Promises to give away large amounts of money, or expensive material objects like houses and cars, are always popular. If you promise to give away a million dollars to a lucky fan if someone hits a grand slam in the fifth inning, or performs some other unlikely feat, you can always buy insurance to cover the prize (see Chapter 5 for more on this). This, too, is a popular event—and less heart-stopping for management if someone else guarantees the payoff. John Tull of the South Bend White Sox once convinced a car dealer to give away a car if someone hit a grand slam in the third inning—and the car dealer was going it alone with no insurance. Sure enough, a kid comes up in the third with the bases loaded, and pops one right over the left field fence: his first pro home run was going to cost this car dealer a cool $20,000. The fans were going completely nuts, especially the one who held the winning ticket stub, the team's management was thrilled because they were going to get the great publicity—come to a South Bend game and go home with a car!—and the car dealer must have been making plans to skip town. Unfortunately for everyone except the car dealer, the kid was so excited by his big hit that he passed the runner in front of him and was called out. No grand slam, no car, no publicity, and one very relieved car salesman.

The Frederick Keys, in Frederick, Maryland, hold an Old-timers' game once a year. This is of course familiar from the big leagues' version of this promotion, but Lupton adds a baseball-card show before the game, charging sellers $100 for a table. The card-show people are happy with this because the event draws 5,000 to 7,500 fans, which is more than they usually get for such things. A minor-league team usually can't get the really big names for their old-timers' games—Joe DiMaggio and Willie Mays don't usually turn up in places like Appleton, Wisconsin. But you can put together enough former major and minor leaguers to make up a couple of teams and have some fun.

There are certain promotions, I've learned, you should never get involved in. Here's a short list of ones I try to stay away from:

1. Anything involving live animals. Greased pigs, giving away ponies, animal races. This always results in embarrassment at best, disaster at worst.

2. Giveaways of anything throwable. Don't give away frisbees, seat cushions, or free food. They'll all wind up on the field or hitting another fan in the head. Baseballs are okay. Kids don't throw those away.

3. Eating contests and free beer nights. I don't have to go into detail on what either of these results in.

4. Amateurs who volunteer to sing the "National Anthem." Unless you like holding your breath in suspense until the aspiring singer hits that "land of the free" line.

One thing no minor-league team can ever promote is winning baseball. Of course, some teams win more than others, but if a team is really good, the most likely thing to happen is that guys will start getting called up—there goes your winning team. But the minors may be the only place left where you can honestly say that winning isn't everything. In fact, it's usually irrelevant. Dave Carl, who's Director of Sales and Marketing for the Tacoma Tigers (despite their name, they're the Triple-A affiliate of Oakland, not Detroit) reminded me that his team lost its first ten games this year. "If we were any better, we'd be shitty," he confided. Yet attendance set an all-time record, prompted in part by a slick advertising campaign with the slogan: "Pure Baseball. Nothing Artificial Added." Their market research told them that, contrary to what the previous owners had believed, their audience was right in the middle of advertiser heaven: the 25- to 44-year-old group. And they packed them in every night—playing consistently lousy baseball all season long.

The majors promote their star players. No minor-league team can ever do this. The minute you have a star and start to promote him, off he goes to the next level or up to the Show. It may be a surprise to people who've only followed baseball in the major leagues, but for a minor-league owner, the players are probably the least important aspect of the team's operations.

Promotion doesn't end when the season ends, either. Minor-league teams, just like major-league teams, operate all year long—there's plenty to keep people busy even when there aren't any games going on. Besides the constant advance sales of tickets and advertising, many teams hold promotions in the winter just to remind people that baseball still exists and will be back before you know it. The Midland Angels in the Texas League, for example, hold a sports banquet and memorabilia auction every January as a benefit for the Special Olympics (and not incidentally as a reminder that they'll be back in the spring). They have a free baseball clinic before the banquet, which they promote at schools. Usually, they can get some major-league players to participate—Bobby Valentine, then the manager of the parent Texas Rangers,

Randy Velarde of the Yankees, and Mike Timlin of the Blue Jays (all Midland-area natives) came last year. They held the banquet at a local country club (they always try to patronize advertisers whenever possible), and sell tickets to the banquet itself. This covers the cost of the room and the meal. What they make on the auction goes to the charity—more than $10,000 for the auctions held in 1990 and 1991 went to the Special Olympics. They auction off autographed baseballs and bats, autographed game jerseys from major-league players, even an item of basketball or football memorabilia if it comes their way—for example, they sold an autographed game jersey of Xavier McDaniel that Knicks head coach Pat Riley had donated to the event, and a football that Earl Campbell had autographed.

Concessions

In case you thought otherwise, this is not just a matter of cooking up a few hot dogs and making sure there's enough mustard to cover them with. Souvenirs and food are a profit center for all teams, and no minor-league team can make a profit without them.

John Tull of the Midwest League South Bend White Sox points out that every penny counts, and the smallest details are important. For example, you probably take hot dogs for granted—you come out to the park, you get a hot dog. It's a reflex. But for John Tull, hot dogs are—I can't think of a better word—thought-provoking. A case of hot-dog wrappers costs $30.00—3 cents a piece. The buns are 6 cents each.

The hot dogs themselves cost 17½ cents, so the little wrappers increase your cost over the plain hot dogs and buns by more than 12%. This is, indeed, food for thought.

So hot dogs—with wrappers and buns—cost you 26½ cents. How do you decide what to price them at? If you've ever been to a major-league game and paid $4.50 for a little cup of warm flat beer, you're probably wondering how they come up with these prices too. A minor-league operator has to be a little more sensitive to price than that. He looks around his neighborhood and sees what others are charging for the same thing. He allows himself a little space because, after all, this is a ball park and not a restaurant. He considers how much of the concession money has to be paid to the city as part of his agreement on the lease (a common clause in stadium-lease agreements), he thinks about what he charged last year, and whether he can maintain that price. He thinks about what he's going to have to charge next year—he wants to leave himself someplace to go when the new season starts with new and bigger expenses.

At South Bend, the city takes roughly 15% of all income from concessions. The state sales tax takes another 5%. So that 20% comes out of the selling price at the top. Tull figures his cost should be no more than 30% of his selling price, so with hot dogs, it comes out like this: If he charges $1.25, less the 20% for the government, times his cost of 26½ cents (wrapper included), his cost is 26.5% of his selling price, so he's in good shape. But there are other considerations. The local 7-11 is selling more or less the same product for 99 cents. Most people wouldn't think of going to a ballgame and not buying at least one of them, so maybe the market will bear a slightly higher price. He did fine last year at $1.50, so he doesn't have to worry that people will complain about a price increase. All things considered, Tull decides that this year, hot dogs will go for $1.50—this gives him a comfortable food cost of 23% of the selling price, and he can still brag that hot dogs cost the same this year as last.

Beer, as you might have guessed, is the biggest money-maker in the food stands, and the item that will bear the highest price. Beer costs the South Bend team about 2 cents an ounce. The 24-ounce cup, which holds 22 ounces of beer and two ounces of foam—costs 10 cents, and they sell the cup of beer for $3.00, an 18% food cost sure to warm the heart of the team's accountant at the end of the season. The price went up from last year's $2.75, but no one seemed to notice: one out of every three fans who walked through the turnstiles at Coveleski Stadium last year bought a large beer and not a single one of them complained about the price.

You may imagine that thinking about hot-dog wrappers and the foam on top of a 22-ounce cup of beer is no way for an adult to spend time, but in fact thoughts like these are essential in making a minor-league operation work. The South Bend team is profitable at least partly because John Tull pays attention to the details.

Advertising sales

The typical Class-A team makes about $50,000 on their program advertising, $100,000 on signs along the fences, $50,000 from radio advertising, and $2,000 from selling the space on the backs of tickets. When I owned South Bend, I decided to charge $3,500 for fence signs at a time when the rest of the league was getting about $1,200. $3,500 was as much as some Triple-A teams were getting, but it worked out well—there was always a waiting list for outfield signs. Now things have gotten a lot more expensive in most places, but at the time, advertising hadn't been sufficiently exploited as a source of income for these organizations.

Today, this is a big part of the income of any team, and all successful teams have aggressive advertising sales representatives who sell space in the signs on the walls of the stadium, in the program, and, for the teams that have them, on the stadium message boards next to the scoreboard. The Salt Lake City Trappers, for example, are successful at least partly because they approach advertising sales with an aggressive professionalism worthy of organizations ten times their size. The Trappers average 5,900 fans per game, and they aren't shy about selling that audience to advertisers.

The Trappers' advertising salespeople, like many minor-league teams, use a slick four-color brochure to tell the world what's for sale. The fence signs, of course, are prime territory for advertisers, and the Trappers' management points out to potential clients that these signs are not only seen by the thousands

who come to the ballpark, but often appear in newspaper photos and local TV coverage for extra exposure. For $2,000, plus a $250 production fee (don't
forget that someone has to pay the guy who paints
the thing) you can buy an 18-foot by 10-foot full-color
sign and for one year advertise anything you want,
provided it's legal. These are the signs that appear
along the outfield wall in fair territory, where neither
you nor the TV and newspaper photographers can
miss them. $1,000 will buy you two 3-foot by 8-foot
signs along the foul lines—one on each side of the
field—and the production fee for these is only $150.
When Roger Kahn and I were part of the Utica Blue
Sox operation, the noted artist John Alexander was
one of our partners. John rented a sign in the outfield
which read "John Alexander, Painter." People were
always calling him up to try to get him to paint their
houses.

The Salt Lake City Trappers' souvenir program is a
professionally produced four-color 11″ × 14″ tabloid,
and space is for sale here too, ranging from $350 for
a one-quarter page black-and-white ad, up to $1,500
for the back cover. Production fee, if the ad isn't cam-
era ready, is $100. Then there's the message board,
where one two-line spot per game for the season will
cost $1,850. And if that's not enough, you can have
the public-address announcer say three sentences
on your behalf between innings at every game. Based
on one spot per game, you'll pay $1,850 for the privi-
lege.

The South Bend White Sox are also among the
more aggressive sellers of advertising—the department is run by Rita Baxter, the wife of John Baxter,

who is President of the team. Rita has been in base-ball for only five years, but she's obviously a quick study. Class-A South Bend's advertising revenues compare favorably with many Triple-A teams. Like most teams, South Bend sells signs, pages in the program, and space in the yearbook. They also sell space on a newly-erected three-sided electronic sign. They sell announcements during the game: for exam-ple, a car wash pays to have its name mentioned when the cleanup hitter comes up for his first at-bat (*clean-up*—get it?). They convinced a car dealership to promise a free car to a selected ticket holder if the 4th batter in the 5th inning hits a grand slam. (No, no cars have changed hands yet.) Baxter says they'll sell just about anything that isn't nailed down—and there's no shortage of customers. All the signs were sold before opening day, and advertising revenues have increased every year since they started five years ago.

According to Baxter, there are a couple of factors that make the South Bend advertising program suc-cessful. First, they have four sales reps who sell ad-vertisers hard. The team promotes games aggressively, so advertisers know they are going to be getting the exposure they're paying for. They keep a clean stadium, and fresh paint on the signs so that an advertiser can be assured that his product ap-pears in the right kind of environment. And of course, they can promise the numbers: More people come to South Bend's Coveleski Stadium to watch baseball every year.

7

Buying the Team

All your other bills are paid. You've decided to put some money into minor-league baseball. Where do you get the cash to do it, and where do you start?

Getting to know minor-league baseball

First, it's important to soak up the atmosphere. Get a subscription to *Baseball America* and *Baseball Today.* These are the trade journals of the industry. They contain information about the industry that you can't get anywhere else. Everyone in baseball reads them, and you should too.

Go to games. When you buy some shares in an oil company, it probably isn't important to go down to the Gulf of Mexico to check out an offshore oil platform—you wouldn't know what you were looking for anyway. But baseball's different: you're a fan, and you know exactly what you're looking for—so go see if the team you're interested in is providing it.

There are minor-league teams all over the country, and one or more of them is within driving distance of your home. So take a look at a few of them—it's a dirty job, but someone's got to do it. All right, this isn't exactly work, but you have to keep your eyes open and note your own reactions in a systematic way. You've probably been to plenty of games, but this time you're looking at the place with a critical eye. A minor-league team thrives only when someone is paying attention to the details. As a potential investor, you should make sure the details are being taken care of. Is it easy to buy a ticket? Are the lines too long at the concession booths? Are the restrooms clean? Are the personnel polite? Does the place make you feel like dropping a few bucks on beer and souvenirs? Is the management attentive to the customers—that is, do they make you want to come back and see another game? In other words, is this a place where you want to spend your free time? If you don't like being there, maybe there's something wrong. Do you see things that ought to be fixed? Do you have any idea of how to fix them? Is this team doing all it can to get more customers into the ballpark?

Often the places that are functioning the best may not have the best investment potential. For an investor, some defects may be a good thing—it means there's room for improvement and that means there's room for your investment to grow. Eric Margenau's strategy is to look for teams that are undervalued. A poor facility or obviously inadequate management are exactly what he's looking for—these are the teams he feels he can buy at a good price and then turn them around to make them worth more than he paid for them.

Eric checks out the market very carefully, too. If this isn't a city where he feels baseball can thrive—if the local government is uninterested, if the population is too small, if the potential for developing the team in this location isn't there, he wants to make sure he can move the team to a better location. Teams in bad locations can be a good buy—provided you can convince the league that moving the team is beneficial to all concerned.

Once you've learned a few things about how minor-league baseball works, you're ready to talk to some minor-league baseball operators. The numbers at the back of this book can put you in touch with hundreds of people willing to talk to you about baseball—in fact, with some of them it's impossible to get them to stop talking! So you don't have to feel that you're trying to get in touch with the president of IBM—these people are, for the most part, perfectly accessible, and you won't have any difficulty in speaking with them.

There's a list of league presidents in the back of this book, too, and it's there for a reason: it's important for any potential investor to get to know these people. They're the ones who will be instrumental in deciding whether you're the right kind of investor in the first place. They'll be the ones you appeal to for permission to move the team if that becomes necessary. They make, and enforce, the rules that make a league function smoothly, and their opinions count.

Next, you'll want to speak with brokers like Bob Richmond, and lawyers like Rich Hill or Art Hittner who have been involved in making deals for minor-league teams. Richmond is especially important in this regard, since he's one of the people who knows the range of what's available, and knows how to put buyers and sellers together. Eventually one or more of these people—or others very much like them—will play an essential role in closing the deal for the team.

Sale price

How do you figure out what a team is really worth? Even a team that isn't making much money has a value. The franchise itself is rare—they're only 150 or so in the whole world, so each one has a value even apart from whatever it may be worth compared to any other business of similar profitability. Remember that this is a world that has a fixed supply but a growing demand: the perfect formula for rising prices, which is exactly what has happened over the last decade.

There are several ways to arrive at a team's value. The first is called stick value—the value that even a team with a poor location, a bad facility, and a bad operating history, will automatically have. Under these circumstances, the ordinary methods of evaluating a business can turn out to be of minimal relevance.

Earnings are the next consideration in estimating

price. As little as five years ago, this would have been put at roughly five times earnings. Today, teams sell for ten times earnings and up.

Finally, some franchises come with a premium, for one reason or another. The Durham Bulls are just an A-league team in the Carolina League, but they have a value far greater than most of the teams in their league. The Salt Lake City Trappers are a premium team as well—their attendance is remarkable, their teams are consistently winners, and their promotion and publicity are superb. They've built themselves into a premium franchise, even though they're an independent team playing at the rookie level. The South Bend White Sox are another example of a team that will command a premium—high attendance, a beautiful stadium, and a sports-addicted market are the reasons. The Buffalo Bisons are perhaps the model of the premium franchise. This Triple-A team has by far the largest attendance of any team in the minors, and they play in a stadium that is, for all practical purposes, a major-league facility.

Where do you get the money to do this? Of course, if you're loaded with money, you just write a check. For a $1 million team, that will be at least $550,000 in cash, because the debt-equity ratio in minor-league ball cannot exceed 45-55. More likely, you'll be part of a group that gets together to do this: a realistic minimum for a share as a limited partner in such an undertaking today would be $25,000.

It's hard, though not impossible, to borrow money for an investment like this. But in general, this isn't the sort of business you would want to come into with a lot of debt to service—operating revenues are difficult enough to produce without having to spend them on interest payments. It's much more sensible in every way to go into this with the money in hand.

The PBA and the rules governing control interest

Having the money is not enough. Rule 36 of the Professional Baseball Agreement is very specific—eight pages of single-spaced typing are required to spell out all the requirements that have to be fulfilled before control interest can be transferred.

First, you have to tell certain people that you're going to start this transaction: the Commissioner of Baseball, the President of the National Association and the league president all have to know about it. And, no, a simple phone call is not enough. Any documents pertaining to the sale, including nonbinding memorandums or letters of intent, have to be turned over to these three offices. It's the President of the National Association who makes the determination about whether the transaction represents a transfer of control interest, and he's the one who notifies the club of his decision.

If it is decided that a control interest transfer is about to take place, the first requirement is a $5,000 payment to the National Association to cover the expenses of the security investigation. The league office will need the names of and biographical information on all those who will have an equity interest in the club. They'll also want a proposed operating budget covering the next three years, and personal financial statements from all concerned, including copies of individuals' tax returns.

Baseball is concerned with the kinds of businesses its owners operate outside of baseball, so they ask each potential owner to disclose any business in which he holds a 5% or greater interest. Certain businesses are singled out for disclosure if a potential owner has any interest at all in them: professional sports, broadcasting, entertainment, cable TV, and, most important, any gambling or gambling-related industry. It is expressly stated in the agreement that the President of the league "shall disapprove any transfer of any interest in a minor-league club to a person or entity which has *any* ownership interest in or management ties to legalized gambling activities." Broadcasting interests are looked at carefully because baseball wants to avoid any conflict of interest in the sale of broadcasting rights to a team's games. They'll want to eliminate a situation in which an owner also owns another team, or even part of another team, in the same league as the one he's proposing to buy. The president will very likely reject any arrangement in which the assets of one team are pledged to secure the loan to buy another team. He will cast a cold eye on any business arrangement like government ownership or nonprofit ownership that might impede sound operations. Even your relatives can be brought into the picture. The league president will consider whether ownership of a team by a relative of another owner would create an unacceptable conflict of interest.

If you're planning to move the franchise, you have to state that up front. And if you're planning to keep it where it is, you have to demonstrate that you have strong ties to the local community, which minor-league baseball rightly considers essential to assuring solid fan support and long-term local government support.

The details of the financing, including the names of all lenders and underwriters is also required. And finally, a good catchall: "any additional information that the President of the National Association may reasonably request." That ought to cover it!

All this applies to all leagues. But some have rules of their own. Some, for example, may lean toward investors who are famous, others might not. Leagues can require different kinds of equity arrangements. They can dictate who will be allowed to function as general or limited partners. It can cost as much as $50,000 in legal and accounting fees just to find out if your entity is acceptable to the National Association and to the league you're trying to buy into. Ten years ago, things were much more informal—but then there was less money involved than there is now.

Any transaction requires the approval of all three levels: the league to which the team belongs, the National Association office, and the Office of the Commissioner of Major League Baseball. I'll leave it to you to imagine the cost of paper and xeroxing that this involves!

Due diligence

This is the period of investigation that precedes the sale of any business, and, as in any business, it's useful to have the help of professionals who are familiar with the ins and outs of the industry.

This is your chance to take the balance sheets the seller has given you and really substantiate them. Say I'm looking at a team whose balance sheet shows a profit of $100,000 for the last year of operation. But in looking over the books, I notice that the payroll isn't enough to cover the number of employees they claim to have. What's wrong? Then I see it: the owner's wife and sister both work for the club for nothing. There's nothing wrong with this, of course, but my wife and sister aren't going to work for the club—I'm going to have to pay two full-time people to fill those positions. There goes the $100,000 profit.

There are many other places to look for profit that may not turn out to be reproducible when you take over. For example, is the guy who sells hot dogs to the team related to the owner? Is he selling hot dogs at a lower price than you could expect to pay? Maybe the seller is getting the hot dogs for free because he traded an advertisement in the program for them— this could radically reduce your food cost, but you might not be able to make the same deal.

Don't forget that minor-league baseball is largely a cash business. This means you have to carefully reconcile the records of expenses and revenues to the deposits and withdrawals recorded on bank statements. You don't have to be terribly cynical to realize that there are plenty of opportunities for fooling around, as well as ample room for innocent error, when a business puts thousands of dollars in cash into a box every night and carries it to the bank.

There are many sophisticated ways to present financial data so that it looks better than it really is. For example, suppose an operator owns four different teams, only one of which—the one you're buying—doesn't make money. It's easy enough for him to write off some of the losses of one team that isn't doing well against the profits of the teams that are. This is an easy way to make the team he's selling look as if it's doing okay when it's really not.

In Chapter 5, I showed you how a typical team might get certain services by barter. You have to be sure of what services the team got this way, and of how that affects their report of expenses. If they've been offering advertising to a bus company to pay for their team's transportation, that's something you should learn in the due diligence period. If they've gotten free landscaping in exchange for a buyout night at the stadium for the landscaping company, that's important in your consideration of their expense ledgers. Each time there's a transaction like this, you have to evaluate it. Can you do the same thing? Do you want to? How much extra should you add to the expenses because of transactions like this? The answers to these questions are going to tell you something about what this team is truly worth.

The lease on the ballpark is always a central issue. This is likely to be the biggest expense, and the leases can be fairly complicated. You'll undoubtedly need a lawyer familiar with the baseball industry to help you read and evaluate this document. Evaluating the ballpark itself is also essential, and it may be useful to get to know local political officials to determine their attitude toward the team, and whether there is the possibility of getting them to help in park improvements. This becomes more and more essential as the new Professional Baseball Agreement standards start to be enforced.

The sales contract

Since almost everyone agrees that the price of a team is dependent on the factors I've mentioned above, and since it's perfectly clear to all concerned which factors apply in any given case, it's pretty hard for a buyer to go into a negotiation with the hope of reducing the price to any significant extent. The status quo supports prices at a certain level, and no individual deal is likely to make them change much.

This leaves everything else to consider, however, which can be quite a bit. The stadium lease and the existing Player Development Contract with the major league team may be the most important element next to price when a team is sold. The value of the lease— or if in fact it has any value—has to be carefully determined. If there are defaults under the stadium lease, these have to be disclosed and settled before the sale can be finalized. It has to be clear that the parent club will continue the existing Player Development Contract—without it, of course, the team may not be worth buying at all.

There is plenty of property that goes along with a team, and all this must be spelled out in the contract

117

of sale. In general, a team will own its office equipment—tables, desks, chairs, copiers, fax machines, computers, file cabinets—and all this is specified as included in the sale. The team may own broadcasting equipment or fixtures like bleachers, concession stands, cooking equipment, and air conditioners. An estimate of their worth, too, is pertinent to the price. The same is true of equipment used to maintain the field. This can add up to quite a bit: rakes, line markers, mowers, blowers, tractors, hoses, shovels, ladders, trailers, seeders, hoes, and air pumps, not to mention the stuff more familiar to fans like pitching screens, batting cages, bases, pitching rubbers, tarps, and—don't forget the essential stuff—home plate.

When Everything
Goes Right

My first team was the Utica Blue Sox, but that wasn't really an investment. I went into that one with Roger Kahn mostly for fun, or at least more as a literary enterprise than a financial one. I didn't expect to make any money on that—and my expectations were fully realized. But a year after selling the team, I missed being around the ballpark. Miles Wolff brought on shareholders in 1983 for $25,000 each. He sold to the present ownership for $75,000 a share. Today, I would say the franchise is worth more than $1 million.

In any case, now I was involved in minor-league ball, and I understood at least a little bit about the way it worked. I'm not saying I was the most sophisticated of investors, but I did have some notion about how money is made and lost in owning baseball teams. And I could see the potential in these organizations as money-makers. My friend Eric Margenau and I decided to go shopping.

The Blue Sox are in the New York-Penn League, a Class-A league that operates mainly in New York State, with a few teams across the river in Ontario, one in Massachusetts, and one in Pennsylvania. You may not recognize the name of a team like the Auburn Astros, but you will know some of Auburn's alumni: Joe Pepitone, Lonnie Smith, Rick Dempsey, Jerry Koosman, Ozzie Virgil, and Mel Stottlemyre all played here before going on to the majors. And other teams in the league have alumni just as distinguished—Wade Boggs played for Elmira, Ken Boyer for Hamilton, Sal Maglie for Niagara Falls, and John Elway—yes, that John Elway—played for Oneonta before he decided to use his throwing arm in other ways.

So the New York-Penn league was the league we knew, and we looked around for a team that was for sale—and that we could afford. This was in 1986, and, although there were certainly some expensive teams around, the big runup in prices was still in the future. The team we set our sights on was the Watertown Pirates.

Watertown had a lot of negatives. Its attendance figures were not healthy. Its home field was a fairgrounds where someone had once laid out a baseball field. The grandstands, such as they were, must have been built for something other than the baseball field, because they were so far away you needed binoculars to make out the pitching mound. In fact, today such a field would never be approved by the

National Association, and no member team would be allowed to play with such a setup. When we decided to buy, we knew that our first act as the new owners would be to find a place for these guys to play—and we pretty much knew it wouldn't be in Watertown.

After plenty of to-ing and fro-ing, Margenau and I made a deal to buy the team for $125,000. That doesn't sound like much money today for a Class-A team, but at that time, no team in the league had sold for more than $75,000. So we paid top dollar. But things were changing rapidly. Within a year after our purchase, the Elmira Pioneers, a Red Sox affiliate, had been sold for something over $300,000.

Eric was (and still is) a psychologist with a thriving private practice. I'd represented Eric on a book he published about sports psychology, so I knew he was a sports fan. In fact, he'd worked for the New Jersey Nets as a consulting psychologist at one point, where he'd gotten his introduction to the whole world of professional athletes. When I approached him about getting into baseball, he looked at it partly as further-ing his interest in sports as a professional, but mostly as a hobby. He thought about the money he'd invest as rather like paying for an expensive sports car. He had the money—it was just a question of whether he wanted to blow some of it in this particular way. Can I afford the payments on this toy? The money was all borrowed (which was still possible at that time), so it made it even easier for him—and me.

It was February, 1986 when I first talked to Eric about buying the team. The conversation about it was about ten minutes long, and thirty seconds after hanging up, Eric had decided to go in with me. To both of us, it felt like putting the team on our Master-cards, and then just facing the payments every month. We were friends, I was inviting him out to play some ball, it was a small price (relatively speaking), and we jumped in.

That first season, we had a great time. Didn't make any money, but that wasn't really the point. We played an exhibition game in Cooperstown that season, brought our families out to see some games, had a grand old time. In other words, we got out of it exactly what we expected to get. It wasn't yet a business, so it didn't matter that all we managed to do was break even. But then summer was over, and it was time to go back to real life. Eric went back to practicing psychology, and I went back to running my literary agency.

In the second year of operation, we got lucky: we won the division pennant for the first time in the franchise's history. But our main problem was not winning baseball games. It was finding a new city, and a stadium to play in.

Baseball teams certainly contribute to a city's economy—the National Association says that a Class-A team will bring over $4 million annually into its home city's economy, with the club itself spending between $300,000 and a million. Now this could be said of lots of other businesses, too, so it's hard sometimes to justify the cooperation—the subsidies, to call things by their proper name—that baseball teams expect and get from local governments, particularly in the construction and operation of stadiums. But baseball teams are viewed, correctly in my opinion, as amenities for a city, just as a playground, or a skating rink, or a museum would be. Both politicians and ordinary citizens want baseball in their hometowns, and they're willing to make it easy for teams to locate their operations there. Now, of course, we're living in harder times, and city governments are less willing to spend taxpayer money than they used to be. It's becoming both politically and fiscally unwise to let baseball teams simply have their way. So there's probably less of a free ride than there used to be, and cities are driving harder bargains before they agree to build.

We looked at several different locations—Pittsfield, Massachusetts; Kingston, New York; East Stroudsburg, Pennsylvania. We were almost ready to go to London, Ontario, but they signed a Double-A team just as we were beginning to talk to them. We finally settled on Welland, Ontario.

The setup in Welland isn't really a stadium—it's a nice ball field, but good enough for a short-season A league team. There are some complications when you set up in Canada—their health insurance is expensive for employees, you need working papers for everyone, and everything seems to cost more up there. But the move accomplished its purpose: it made the team profitable, which it hadn't been before.

The year we moved to Welland, the New York-Penn League expanded, and Watertown got a new franchise. The new Watertown owners were successful in persuading local government to improve the facility.

Eric's wife is Canadian, and he has relatives who live right near Welland. So everything was working out fine, and we were both having a great good time.

GREEN DIAMONDS

The South Bend White Sox

Then in the fall of 1987, I found I had a chance to buy another team. The South Bend White Sox, an expansion team in the Midwest League, was available. This team had never played a game, but the present owners were tired of fighting with the city over construction of the stadium, and they wanted out. Unlike the Watertown team, this was a full-season A-league team, and the price was a bit higher: $455,000. Now things were getting serious. Eric and I did a lot more soul-searching, and a lot more research (though not nearly enough, as it turned out) before we decided to go ahead with this one. Getting started there was tough (see Chapter 6 for the complete story of how we dealt with the local government), but once we settled in South Bend, its mayor, and its city officials were extremely helpful in all respects. 1988 was our first season there, and it was tremendously successful. We'd borrowed about $600,000—again, as was permissible then, none of our own money was in the deal—to cover the cost of the team, putting in concessions equipment and other improvements to the stadium, and to have some working capital. We really didn't expect to make any money at this either, but that first year we made enough to cover our debt service and actually have a little left over as profit. The 1989 season was even better. Much to our surprise, we were actually running a business that made money.

But the undertaking was enormous. Eric was devoting more time to it than I was, and his psychology practice—and his income—was starting to suffer. My own business, my agency, wasn't really affected by these other activities. But Eric was taking on a tremendous amount of work, attending team meetings, league meetings, lease negotiations, hiring and firing. Everything that goes into running a business, was falling on his shoulders, and each hour taken up that way was an hour less that he could see patients—which, after all, is how he made a living.

Eric was also having thoughts about whether he wanted to continue in the private practice of psychotherapy. He was getting tired of it—although he says now he didn't realize it at the time—and he was looking for something else to do. Minor-league baseball was beginning to look like more than just a hobby. By the end of the 1988 season, we were both thinking of buying more teams. Things were expanding more rapidly than we had thought they would. At this point, it was clear that our 50/50 arrangement just wasn't fair to Eric, and we had to change it. We created United Baseball, Inc., Eric became head of it, and he started collecting a salary for his work. Maybe I still wasn't a professional baseball operator, but Eric certainly was, and there was no way for him to continue without being paid like a professional.

By this time, Eric was feeling pretty overwhelmed by the work of owning two teams at the same time, each with its own problems, and he had very little help from anyone. Then in August, 1989, an old friend of mine, Alan Levin called. I'd seen him infrequently but regularly over the years. We needed a third hand badly at this point, and Alan was the one we needed.

Alan, before he came into baseball, had been an

executive at CBS—he's also the lawyer who helped me form my first corporation back in the late 1960s—and he had the business expertise we needed. When he saw an article in the paper discussing my plans to put together a new minor league on Long Island, he gave me a call. Alan's a fan of baseball, but not a fanatic. He was interested in baseball as a business proposition, without much of the sentimentality that's often associated with people who get into this field. His specialty is the operational side of a business, and this was the kind of expertise Eric and I needed. It wasn't hard to persuade him to join the fun. He was looking for new challenges, and he quickly realized that running a minor-league team profitably was about as challenging as it could get!

In the fall of 1988, with Alan on board, we bought the Peninsula Pilots—going into the deal with full knowledge that this was a team in considerable trouble, but with the conviction that we could turn it around. The team didn't even have any major-league affiliation, so there was absolutely no way we could make money the first year. We managed to get a Japanese team, the Hiroshima Carp, to send over a half dozen players, a coach, and a translator, and Syd Thrift, then with the Yankees, helped out with a few players for which we were grateful. We managed to lose $200,000 in the 1989 season—but at the same time South Bend was making $400,000. Our Watertown team by this time was settled in Welland, Ontario, and they were starting to be profitable, too. So 1989, despite the problems with the Peninsula Pilots, was a profitable year for United Baseball, Inc. The partnership was working well, each of us contributing skills to an operation that, overall, was making much more money than we ever really thought it would.

By 1990, I was ready to move on to other things, but the South Bend operation was going so well, and Alan was having so much success running it, that he decided to buy us out. The deal included the Welland Pirates as well, now doing nicely up in Canada. The South Bend franchise is now one of the most profitable in the minors. Alan also still owns the Welland Pirates, and, with three other partners, he bought the Modesto A's in the Class-A California League in 1990.

Alan will be the first to admit that it isn't just business genius that makes the South Bend team so successful. There are several other important factors that have nothing to do with management skill. For one thing, Coveleski Stadium is a spectacular facility. Fans want to come to it, and when they do they enjoy being there. The South Bend community—even though the city government gave the team a hell of a time when they were trying to get the stadium built—are a dedicated sports audience. Every Notre Dame home football game attracts 59,075 people, a complete sellout. Attendance at Coveleski last season was over 200,000. And the per-game average has increased every year since the new stadium went up.

I spoke with Alan shortly after he'd returned from the Winter Meetings in 1992. He's now running three successful teams, he understands the business side of minor-league baseball as well as anyone I know, and he's beginning to move in new directions as well. The problem of recruiting good personnel has always been a problem for the minor-leagues. Once, this was a business run part-time, with seasonal help, most of it amateur—even most of the owners were amateurs. But it's not like that anymore. To run a successful operation you need good, dedicated, professional personnel.

As a result, Alan, along with Leanne Pagliai, the general manager and part-owner of the High Desert Mavericks, has started a search firm to match people looking for jobs in sports management with the teams that can use their talents. The company, National Sports Placement, which will serve not just baseball but other pro sports as well, has started with some 450 applicants and over 150 listed jobs. This is the only search firm specializing in the field, and it's going to be a great relief to job seekers to have some organized and dignified way to contact potential employers and find the right job, instead of milling around the halls and hoping to stumble upon the right person at the Winter Meetings.

Alan is also acutely aware of the problem of minority hiring in baseball, and he has plans to try to do something about this problem, through his new venture. The Marge Schott affair, which dominated conversation at the Winter Meetings in 1992, has made everyone in baseball more conscious of the potentially explosive situation faced by the management side of the sport.

Purely as a business proposition—even putting aside abstract questions of social justice—baseball has to reach out to a black audience. Alan reminded me that Coveleski Stadium in South Bend is in a predominantly black neighborhood, but that black faces in the crowd at the stadium are rare. Writing off this market is just plain bad business, yet the tradition of baseball, even after all these years, is still geared toward a white audience. It's one baseball tradition no one in the game wants to preserve.

PART FOUR

Life on the Farm

9

The Players

With the two new expansion teams, there will be about 700 available jobs for major-league ballplayers starting in 1993. I mentioned earlier that there are about 5,500 active minor-league ballplayers. Lots of people wonder how many of these make it to the majors—so much so that *Baseball America* got tired of people calling them up to ask. They decided to do a study and settle the question once and for all. They discovered that about 10.6% of players make it to the majors for even one day. The number who have significant careers in the majors is, of course, much smaller. To put it bluntly, even if a minor leaguer is very good, it's pretty unlikely that he will ever put on a major-league uniform at all, and if he does, it probably won't be for long. It takes a combination of superior skills and the right circumstances. (Does the parent club need a catcher at the moment? Do they already have a power-hitting lefty first baseman? Did this guy offend one of the important people in the player-development office?) For any minor leaguer to go to the Show is tough, and every player who comes into the minors either already knows this, or learns it fast. The sad fact is that the most likely outcome for a minor leaguer is that he'll have a short career, and that all of it will be spent in the minor leagues.

Where do these players come from? Scouts for major-league teams are constantly looking for talent—and not just in this country. The Giants, for example, have twenty-two scouts going all over the hemisphere looking for the best young players. Everyone knows that the Dominican Republic is a rich source of baseball talent, and every major-league team has people scouting the playgrounds of towns like San Pedro de Macoris. Players also come from Central and South America, and scouts travel to Panama, Venezuela, Nicaragua, and other countries where they have found the likes of Roberto Kelly, Andres Gallaraga, and Dennis Martinez. Of course, scouts check out high schools and colleges in the U.S. thoroughly—but it's not always as easy as it seems.

Publications like *Baseball America* and *USA Today*'s *Baseball Weekly* gather plenty of information on the top draft choices, unlike the old days when rumor was the chief source of communication. Teams could easily embarrass themselves this way. There's a story that Cleveland once drafted a player who had actually died some months earlier, which may help to explain what goes on in Cleveland these days. Usually young players are drafted into the rookie or A leagues, but every once in awhile, especially in dealing with more experienced college players, a talented player will find himself in Double-A for his first job in pro baseball.

A minor-league team can have twenty-three players on their active roster. When you draft a very young player, you're taking a chance, not only because baseball talent is hard to judge when a kid is seventeen or eighteen, but also because the major-league team will have to protect a player after four years of minor-league service or risk his becoming eligible to be drafted again. The majors are allowed forty men on their rosters, so they can't always protect everyone they'd like to. Also, minor-league players can now become free agents after six years of service.

But for fans, and certainly for owners, one of the most rewarding aspects of the game is watching a talented young player mature into a major-league ballplayer. I've had this pleasure many times—and, believe me, you can't have it often enough.

Tim Wakefield came to the Watertown Pirates in 1988. He was a weak-hitting first baseman with a decent glove and a medium arm. He spent the entire season with us playing first base, distinguishing himself only by being hit by a pitch nine times. In other words, he looked like a guy who didn't have much of a future anywhere, not even in a Class-A league. He came into his second season with us (we'd moved to Welland by this time) where we switched him around to third for a while, trying to find someplace where he could play. He didn't leave much of an impression there, either. But then something odd

happened. Wakefield was fooling around in the outfield before a game, trying, like many hitters, to show
he could pitch, too. But this guy was throwing something unusual: a looping, twisting, floating, fluttering
pitch that looked as if it was going 50 miles an hour,
tops. And it looked impossible to hit, too. The guy had
that rarest of all pitches: a real live knuckleball. There
are only a couple of pitchers in the majors who throw
a knuckleball at all, and it seemed to everyone that
this was one of the best they'd ever seen. The Pirates
wanted to stick with him. In 1990, he went to Salem,
in the Carolina League, his first shot at a full-season
league, and his first chance to spend an entire season
as a pitcher.

Now the organization was really starting to notice.
He led the league in starts and innings pitched that
year—and also in walks. By 1991, he had moved up
to the Double-A Carolina Mudcats, and then to Buffalo at the end of July for one game, then back again
to Carolina. Minor leaguers have to keep their suit-
cases packed. He started out the 1992 season with
Buffalo, when, finally, in late July, the Pittsburgh Pirates decided they could use a pitcher to stand in for
Zane Smith, whose shoulder was aching. Wakefield
spent the rest of the season baffling National-League
hitters with a 55-mile-an-hour knuckleball, and a
fast ball that gets up to maybe 70 if the wind's behind
him. He wound up with an 8-1 record and a 2.15
E.R.A., a significant factor in taking the Pirates to the
Eastern Division championship. Not bad for a weak-
hitting first baseman who sometimes played third.

Wakefield was twenty-two years old when he came
to play professional ball, as the Pirates' eighth-round

selection in the June, 1988 free-agent draft. He'd been a slugging first baseman in college—set a school record, in fact, for home runs in his career. He batted .344 with 22 homers and 71 RBI in only 189 at bats his last year of college ball. But it shows you how far a college player is away from major-league quality when you consider his dismal performance the next year in A ball. But that, of course, is what the minors are for: to develop a player, to teach, to help him find his talents—talents that, in the case of Wakefield, neither he nor anyone else even knew he had when he first was drafted. Now if the Pirates had made it to the World Series in Wakefield's rookie year ... well, never mind: baseball is real life and that's just not the way real life works. But watching Wakefield pitch the Pirates to two wins in the playoffs against Atlanta in 1992—to play even a small part in that, or even only to watch it happen, is a joy.

That same fall, I watched Orlando Merced in the playoffs playing against Atlanta for the National League Championship. And I could remember his seasons back in 1986 and 1987 with Watertown. He'd come out of American Legion ball in his native Puerto Rico, and this was not a guy who showed much promise, at least to my eye. In '86, he hit .191. In '87, he came to Watertown where he played in four games before he broke his hand and missed the rest of the season. But then in 1988 there was a turning point, the kind you can only really see in retrospect. Still playing in Class-A ball, now at Salem and Augusta, his bat came alive—he had a .450 slugging percentage and a .283 average in 117 games that year. Up to Buffalo he went in July of 1989, where in his first season of Triple-A ball he started off by getting 19 hits in his first 38 times at bat. In 1990, he continued his hot hitting with the Buffalo club, and made three separate appearances in Pittsburgh, all as a pinch hitter. Then he got his shot, and made it work: in 1991, his first full season in the majors, he finished second to Houston's Jeff Bagwell in the voting for Rookie of the Year. Today, he's solidly settled as a legitimate big-league ball player—with two years of post-season play in his first two years in the Show. I like to think I can judge baseball talent, but I have to admit I didn't see any of this in the good-looking Puerto Rican kid who could barely figure out how to use a bat for my short-season A-league club.

Some guys you watch bounce around from one minor-league team to another, ever hopeful that they're going to make it someday. This is probably more typical than the guys who make a direct climb from their first pro job to the major leagues. Mike Maksudian, who played for South Bend in 1988 is an example. He came to our A-league team from Sarasota, the White Sox rookie team in the Florida State League. He did well for us—hit .303 in 102 games. This was enough to convince the Mets that they wanted him, and they traded for him in 1988, sending him to their St. Lucie team. 1989 was another up-and-down year for Maksudian. The Mets released him in March, the independent Miami club in the FSL picked him up in May, and then in December the Blue Jays chose him in the minor-league draft, sending him to their AA team in Knoxville. By 1991, he'd made his way to Syracuse, the Blue Jays Triple-A affiliate in the International League. And in late August of 1992, he arrived in Toronto. He only had three at bats for the season, and didn't get a hit—but hope is still alive: Kansas City picked him up for next year.

Maksudian is a guy you want to root for. He's been kicking around the minors for five years, a hard-nosed catcher with some pop in his bat. And he's a leading candidate for the Bill Lee Spaceman of the Year Award: the guy eats bugs. No kidding. Apparently he's been doing this since he was in rookie ball in Florida. I can't say I ever saw him do this—I'm sure I'd remember it if I had—but according to *USA Today*, his teammates at Toronto took up an $800 collection to watch him eat a 1½-inch-long live locust. Crunched it right down. He's eaten worms, too, and grasshoppers, roaches, and spiders—if it crawls, he'll eat it. *USA Today* quotes him as saying—and again, I'm not vouching for this, because I didn't hear it with my own ears—"It's mind over matter. You try to think of something that tastes good—like strawberries—and then kill it in your mouth as fast as you can so it doesn't jump around." Maksudian says it helped keep the Jays loose during the pennant drive. I guess it worked. After Toronto's spectacular performance in 1992, there are probably a bunch of major-league scouts right now out there checking the rookie leagues for a catcher with a good arm who likes ants for lunch. I hope the majors don't spoil this guy—can you see him going into a free-agent negotiation with his lawyer, his agent, his briefcase, and a bag of cater-pillars for a snack?

Scott Radinsky, the White Sox left-handed set-up man is a guy I saw twice on my teams, first at Peninsula in 1987, when he (with plenty of help from his teammates, I should add) stunk up the league with a 1–7 record and a 6.77 ERA. It was a season that earned him a trip to the Gulf Coast League, where, it was hoped, he'd learn something. It must have worked—he came back to A-ball with my South Bend team in 1989, where he became the best stopper in the league: 31 saves and a 1.75 ERA. The parent club took note: in 1990 he became the first pitcher since Dwight Gooden in 1984 to go directly from Class A to the majors. He had a 6–1 record with the big club that year. In '91 he went 5–5, with a 2.00 ERA and 8 saves, and in 1992 he was 3–7 with 15 saves and a 2.73 ERA. Whatever happens from here on, he's earned a spot in the big leagues—something that looked pretty unlikely the first time I watched him play.

Some players catch your eye from the very start. Back in 1986, when I found out that a twenty-year-old kid named Moises Alou would be coming to my team in Watertown, I knew before even seeing him that he had the right background at the very least. He's from the Dominican Republic, that incredibly rich source of baseball talent. His father Felipe and his uncles, Matty and Jesus, all had long major league careers. Not to mention his brother Jose who played in the Expos' farm system, and his cousin, Mel Rojas, who pitches for the Expos. Everyone knew that this was a major-leaguer in the making. Even so, it would take five years of minor-league ball to get Moises ready to play in the bigs. He had the talent, but this was a guy who would do a 360-degree turn under a fly ball. In fact, he was so fast that it didn't matter—he'd catch up with it anyway—but you could easily see that Moises needed some seasoning. With Watertown, he was off to a good start: his first home run, in his third professional game, was a grand slam. That year he hit .236 for us, and led the league in triples. He played three years of A ball, then two at the AA level. In 1990, he played for Buffalo and Indianapolis at the Triple-A level, and went up to the majors with Pittsburgh, traded later that season to Montreal. Then he sat out 1991 after shoulder surgery, and came back in '92 to hit .282 with the Expos. I can't wait till next year.

10

The Teams

The character and quality of minor-league teams vary widely. Here, I'm going to try to describe a few of the successful teams—teams that are in some sense among the legendary minor-league teams—concentrating especially on the ways they function as businesses. Minor league teams are run by a great variety of people—politicians, Wall Street investors, local businessmen, and lifelong professional baseball men (and a few women)—and everyone runs things in his or her own way. But the teams I'm describing here, whoever their owners are, are all run successfully, and successful teams tend to have a lot in common. They have locations in good markets. They have owners who know how to promote the game. They have the proper facilities for professional baseball. And they all have rabidly loyal fans.

GREEN DIAMONDS

The Durham Bulls

If you asked the average person to name a minor-league baseball team, chances are this is the one that would come to mind—largely because of that movie. Of course, it's only a movie, and you won't find Nuke Laloosh's locker down here in Durham. You will, however, find an animated billboard of a bull that lights up and breathes smoke for every Bulls home run—and often for lesser feats as well. This is truly life imitating art, because the bull was an invention of the movie company—they left it here when they were done shooting. Anyone who comes to see a Bulls game after seeing that movie expects to see the smoke-breathing bull, and one thing a successful team does is give the fans what they expect. Real life is different from the movies as everyone knows, but sometimes it's not all that different. In any case, the movie certainly made the team famous—people from all over the country now write to the Bulls for caps and mugs and T-shirts, so much so that Miles Wolff, until recently the owner of the team, had to set up an 800 number and open a store across the street from the stadium just to take care of the demand.

The producer of the movie, Thom Mount, was one of the Bulls' first investors when Miles Wolff took over the team. Mount always said he wanted to make a baseball movie, and one day he actually did it. Ron Shelton, a former minor leaguer himself, was the screenwriter and director, and the team did what they could to help when the movie people came to town.

The Bulls are a Class-A affiliate of the Atlanta Braves, and even though most people outside of Durham never heard of them before they saw the movie, they were actually a charter member of the Carolina League, established in 1945. Brett Butler and Bob Boone are both alumni; so are Rusty Staub and Mickey Lolich. Wolff moved the team back to Durham in 1979 after buying it for $2,500—essentially the fee to join the league—and getting the city to refurbish their old stadium. He opened the 1980 season there, and their games soon became regular sellouts. So, to be fair, they were a successful club before the movie was released, though maybe not quite so successful as they are now. They draw over a quarter of a million fans a year—not bad for a team that plays seventy home games a year in a stadium that holds 5,000 people. If the New York Yankees filled the same percentage of available seats that the Bulls fill, their yearly attendance would be somewhere around 3.5 million. When Wolff sold the Bulls to Jim Goodmon, a broadcast executive in Raleigh, for $4 million, he was probably getting a fair price.

It wasn't always like this. In June, 1981, Wolff wrote an article in *Inside Sports* about his first year with the Bulls—"When the Lights Went Out in Durham." He describes a situation that was pretty typical for the time. It was October, 1979, when there hadn't been any movies about the minors, and the bush leagues were really bush, that Wolff took over the team. Wolff hustled his friends and family for $30,-000 in working capital, and went to work wondering whether he'd make any money at all during the season. The city demanded the stadium rent for the entire season up front—not exactly a vote of confidence. The advertisers he'd lined up all wanted to wait until opening day before they paid their bills. The grass in the outfield was brown, and the nice new uniforms Wolff had bought for the team were stolen the day before the opener. The Braves, then and still now the parent club of the Bulls, came up with some used Braves uniforms so the team wouldn't have to play in its underwear, but there was no insurance on the stolen clothes, and certainly no guarantee that there'd be enough money in the kitty to pay for new uniforms when they were delivered six weeks later.

This was only the beginning of the problems. On April 15 of that first season, half the lights went out in the sixth inning of a game, and the water stopped running in the bathrooms. The health department didn't like the condition of the concession stand, and they were threatening to close it down if the Bulls didn't buy a lot of expensive equipment to bring it up to standard. Fortunately, they allowed it to stay open—lots of beer was being sold, despite the 45-degree temperature at game time, and the money would come in handy.

Then the team started doing well, and by the middle of May, Wolff was actually making money, with crowds averaging 2,000 a game. The Bulls were beginning to develop the college crowd that has kept them profitable ever since. Needless to say, beer was a big part of their success at drawing fans—North Carolina had finally loosened up its liquor laws enough to allow beer to be sold at stadiums, and the Bulls were taking full advantage of the new regulations. Wolff says that the mix of fans was broad—college kids, blue collar workers, women, blacks, and plenty of kids. He even claims—and I don't know whether to believe this one or not—that there was a blind guy who would come to the games with a friend and boo the umpires right along with everyone else.

Things were going well enough in Durham, but there were a few weak spots in the rest of the league that Wolff had to concern himself with that first year. The Rocky Mount Pines were about to fold, and there's no way a league can go on with seven teams instead of eight. You'd lose ten home dates, which in the minors—and this is still true today—can mean the difference between a profitable season and losing your shirt. So the other teams had to chip in to prop up the Pines at least through the end of the season.

But in the end all the travails were worth it. Wolff wasn't interested in getting rich (though I guess he eventually did) and he was thrilled to have a winning team that the fans loved.

The Toledo Mud Hens

No doubt about it: this team has the best name of any sports team in the universe. Well, all right. I'll allow fans of the Quad City River Bandits in the Midwest League and the Albany Polecats in the South Atlantic League to have their say, too. Here's another team made famous in fiction—this time by a TV show. When Corporal Max Klinger on "MASH" spent the entire Korean War keeping up to date on the scores of Toledo Mud Hens games, the team got more attention than it had ever received before. There was a Toledo minor-league franchise from 1902 to 1955, but the present Mud Hens, members of the International

League, didn't come into existence until 1965. They've been around ever since, affiliated with the Tigers as their Triple-A farm team since 1989. Klinger's team has been an exercise in futility as far as winning games in the International League—they've only won one league championship in all those years. But Klinger must have admired their list of alumni: Casey Stengel, Mike Marshall, Tim Teufel, Kirk Gibson, and Frank Viola among other major leaguers, all played for Toledo. And I guess you could count Kirby Puckett as a former Hen, since he spent a month with the club when it was a Twins affiliate. Maumee, the suburb of Toledo where the Mud Hens play, is only sixty miles from Detroit—though it sometimes seems further than that for the players here who are waiting to go to the bigs.

The Mud Hens are a public nonprofit operation owned by Lucas County. The Mud Hens' attendance—and their won-lost record—are both the worst in the International League. In 1991, they came in second from the bottom in attendance, and dead last in the standings. But they've made plenty of money selling souvenirs. In fact, they can tell when reruns of "MASH" start playing in foreign countries—the orders for Mud Hens paraphernalia start pouring in from abroad.

Toledo has a long history in baseball, dating all the way back to 1883, when the first professional baseball team took up residence there. Needless to say, that team doesn't have much to do with the present Mud Hens—continuity in these things is hard to come by. But it's fair to say that Casey Stengel was one of Toledo's most successful managers, starting with the team in 1926.

The Lucas County Recreation Center was built in 1963, and Ned Skeldon, a local civic leader, acquired a franchise from Richmond two years later. Since 1965, the Hens have changed affiliations regularly—they've been with the Yankees, the Phillies, the Indians, the Twins, and now the Tigers. Watching games at Lucas is a real pleasure—it really has the feel of an old-time minor-league park.

The Salt Lake City Trappers

This is one of the very few independent teams in the minors—not affiliated with any major-league team. The team is owned by sixteen partners, one of whom is the comedian Bill Murray. It's very tough to stay in existence these days without major-league affiliation, but the Trappers have managed to do it—in various incarnations, and for varying periods of time, to be sure—since the 1930s. They do it by signing players the regular draft ignores—scouting them themselves, unlike affiliated teams who take what the parent club gives them. They've been under the current ownership since 1985, playing in the Pioneer League, a short-season rookie-classification league, the first step for many players on the long road to the majors. The Trappers became famous in 1987 for setting a minor league record: they won twenty-nine games in a row. In 1992, their attendance was well over 200,000 for their thirty-five home games in Derks Field—more than twice as many as any other team in the league, and a per game average higher than most Triple-A teams.

I asked Miles Wolff, the publisher of *Baseball America* and the former owner of the Durham Bulls, why it was that the Trappers, an independent team with no major-league subsidies, managed to consistently turn a profit. His answer was simple: "They play good ball, and they win." The Trappers—and any other independent team that's run well—don't have to keep players who aren't playing well, and they don't have to watch their best players taken away and moved around by a parent club. According to Wolff, there is plenty of baseball talent out there—he points out that 200 men play in the College World Series, and the draft takes about twenty of them. That leaves 180 talented athletes for independent teams to pick from, and if they know what they're doing, they're going to come up with some good ones. These guys may not all be big-league prospects, but they're certainly Double-A prospects, and a Double-A prospect can put on a damned good show on a baseball field. That's what Trapper fans get when they come—in droves—to Derks Field.

With Hollywood owners, a feature on the "Today Show," and a general manager who keeps urging Bill Murray to wear a Trappers T-shirt in a movie to improve his concessions sales, the Trappers may be just one notch too worldly to represent baseball like it used to be. This is a money-making enterprise, though, and any impression of lack of sophistication is probably generated by their own publicity department. The general manager, Dave Baggott, a former minor-league player himself, is well-practiced in the art of the interview, and a shrewd promoter of his team. He's on first-name terms with Deedee Corradini, the mayor of Salt Lake City, a relationship that serves him well: the Trappers are due for a new stadium next year, and he needs all the political allies he can get.

Most minor-league teams have some coverage of their games on radio, but the Trappers are one of only a handful that have obtained TV coverage. Dave Baggott showed me some of the tapes, and the production is first-rate. Understand that this is the minors, still—we're not talking about putting the entire season on a local TV station, or getting CBS to televise a Game of the Week. In fact, the Trappers only televised six of their games, two live and four on tape delay, and the broadcasts went no further than the state of Utah. But cable stations are desperate for sports, and a rookie-league baseball game—any rookie-league game—is obviously a better draw than a junior-college volleyball tournament. Baggott found an independent producer who owns a TV production facility in a trailer, and was willing to produce the show for $2,000 a game. Like most minor-league operators, Baggott views a broadcast as a giant advertisement for his team, and whatever money he clears on selling advertising is just gravy.

Derks Field is falling apart. Literally. Last year the city had to condemn 1,500 seats—good seats, too, from the point of view of seeing the action on the field—as too dangerous to let people sit in. You'd get a good view, said the engineers, as long as you didn't fall through the seat, which was a distinct possibility. Every local paper, every local radio and TV station

151

had pieces on the mess at Derks—it was falling down (shot of run-down entrance to the park), it was dangerous (shot of rotting seat), it was hardly a place you'd want to take a family to a ball game (shot of nice clean family). This is exactly what a team needs right before the start of a season when they're trying to sell some seats. But Trappers management are not the kind of people who panic—everything can be turned around, if you know how to do it, which the Trappers do.

First, they reminded everyone the stadium was not falling down, that none of the engineers who checked the place out claimed it was in any way dangerous to go there, that there would be a certain number of seats roped off during the season, but that the stadium itself was fine. Then the fun began: Baggott and his promotional staff set to work.

For starters, they got the mayor to go on TV and say the park was safe—that it would be the same Derks Field as last year, but with 8,500 seats instead of 10,000. Since the 1,500 seats were already in the news, the team decided to use them—the first 500 people to show up on opening day would get a T-shirt that said "I Survived Derks Field," and a construction helmet with the same inscription. The seats were covered with a green tarp, so they cut holes in it, and put mannequins in the "seats." They cut some more holes, and had a promotion in which every time a foul ball fell through one of the holes, a lucky ticket holder would get a prize. It all worked like a dream: the condemned seats became an attraction, and the Trappers set yet another attendance record for the season. And next year comes the new park. Baggott says the city is trying to attract a Triple-A franchise, but they haven't yet, and it looks like the Trappers are going to be the beneficiaries. The Trappers are the very model of a modern minor-league team—sharp, sophisticated, media-wise. It may not be the good old days, but then maybe the good old days weren't that good anyway.

The Buffalo Bisons

Buffalo was one of four cities in the running for getting one of the two new National League expansion teams for the 1994 season, but they lost out to Denver and Miami. Still, getting a big-league franchise may not have been that important after all—Buffalo fans have made this Triple-A Pirates affiliate the single most profitable team in the minor leagues and probably the most valuable minor-league franchise there is. Pilot Field, the 20,050-seat stadium where they play, is a $40-million masterpiece of baseball stadium architecture—people who've seen games there unanimously rate it among the best places in the country to watch baseball.

The Bisons are owned by Robert Rich and his son Robert, Jr. Rich Jr. is President of Rich Products Corporation, a large frozen-food manufacturer. Since 1988 he has also owned the Wichita Wranglers in the Double-A Texas League, and the Niagara Falls Rapids in the Class-A New York-Penn League. He has owned the Bisons since 1984, when Rich Products Corporation bought the Wichita Double-A franchise. In 1987, the Bisons became the Triple-A affiliate of the Cleveland Indians, and then in 1988 began their relationship with the Pirates.

Professional baseball has been in Buffalo for over 100 years, starting with a team organized in 1877. They were the home of major-league teams as well—they had a team in the National League for seven seasons starting in 1879, and in 1890 they joined the Players League (which disappeared after just one season). From 1901 through 1970, Buffalo was a minor-league town in the International League. Then the team closed up and moved to Winnipeg, leaving Buffalo without baseball until 1979, when a group of civic leaders got together to buy a Double-A franchise. This was the team—one with declining attendance figures—that Rich bought in 1983. Rich made an immediate success of the team—so much so that he was able to bring a Triple-A franchise to the city in 1985, moving the Double-A franchise to Wichita. The move to Pilot Field in 1988 was the icing on the cake for a highly successful team—attendance really took off at this point. The Bisons have topped a million in attendance every year since they moved into this facility, and they routinely have higher total attendance figures than two or three major-league teams.

The Memphis Chicks

Bo knows the Chicks—Jackson played fifty-three games there before going to the Show with the Royals in 1986. Since 1984, the Chicks have been the Royals AA affiliate, producing such stars as Jim Eisenreich and Kevin Seitzer for the parent club, as well as David

Cone, Tim Raines, Luis Aparicio, and Ted Kluszewski.

Although Memphis has a long history of professional baseball, there hadn't been a team in the city for more than ten years when Avron Fogelman brought this franchise there in 1979. By the late 1980s, the team was successful enough to get a two-million dollar offer from Craig Stein and Steve Resnick, who owned the team for two years before selling to the present owners in 1989.

The South Bend White Sox

I had to get one of my own teams in this list—the South Bend team may not be legendary in the same sense as the Durham Bulls, but they're as good a team as there is in the minors, and they're worth discussing here. In any business, there are times when everything seems to fall right into place. That was what happened after Eric Margenau and I bought the South Bend White Sox. I recounted the tortuous story of our buying the team. But after that pain came the pleasure of operating a successful business in a town that welcomed baseball. That first year was a losing one on the field—we wound up 22 games under .500—but it was a winning year in every other sense. We drew more than 170,000 fans, second-best in the Midwest League that year. The new stadium was a pleasure to everyone—the owners, the mayor, the citizens of South Bend (especially in the neighborhood around the park), and the tens of thousands of baseball fans who watched the team play.

There were problems, of course. The concession

lines were a problem, especially at the beginning of the season, and we had some difficulties in maintaining the quality of the playing surface. We were pretty amateurish about our promotions—some of them worked, but quite a few just fell flat. But we were learning.

The city was especially pleased with our performance. Joseph Kernan, the new mayor, believes that we had a significant psychological impact as well as an economic one. The downtown area of South Bend became a place people wanted to go to again. Kernan reminded everyone that an Indiana University professor named John Peck had predicted that the Sox would only draw 1,600 per game the first year. When we drew an average of 2,600 per game no one heard much from the professor. The city was the direct beneficiary of this upsurge in attendance, since our lease was based on the city getting a percentage of receipts. We guaranteed them a minimum of $50,000, a figure we reached by the beginning of June, with most of the season left to play.

By the time the season ended, even the local paper, at best a halfhearted supporter of putting the team in South Bend, was an unabashed booster: "This opening year was a grand success," they wrote in an editorial at the end of the season—almost a complete turnaround from eighteen months earlier, when they wondered aloud about whether the mayor had his financial priorities confused when he pushed for building the stadium and establishing a team.

John Baxter was our general manager back then—he's now President of the team—and he stated his aims pretty clearly at the end of that first season: he wanted to make the South Bend franchise as successful as the Louisville or Buffalo operations. In the years since, he's gone a long way toward doing exactly that. 1991's attendance was 221,000, setting yet another record for the franchise.

The Burlington Indians

Miles Wolff owned the Durham Bulls, and, as we know, got rich when he sold them. But he also owns the Burlington Indians, a much less famous rookie-classification team in the Appalachian League—the Appy League, as it's known to everyone in baseball. Burlington, North Carolina is not what Madison Avenue advertising executives are talking about when they discuss "major markets," but from mid-June to the end of August, this league plays a schedule that's about as close as it comes to minor-league baseball in the old days. The 1990 season was typical with Burlington. While Wolff was preoccupied with the goings-on in Durham—it was his last season with the Bulls—the Burlington team was having a mediocre 35–36 season, no better or worse than the Bulls, but when you look at the numbers you get a picture of how slender the profits can get at the lower levels of the minors, even with a relatively successful team like Burlington. The 1990 gross—we're talking about the whole year here, and we're including gate, concessions, and souvenirs—was a little over $125,000. And the team was profitable, making about $15,000 for the year. When you compare this to the half million the Bulls routinely make on concessions alone, though, it's a little depressing. Still, this is pure minor-league ball, and, for the Appy League, the Burlington team is a healthy and successful operation.

PART FIVE

Baseball Owners and Operators: Businessmen and Others

11

The People of Minor-League Baseball

It used to be that the typical minor-league team owner, especially at the Rookie and A levels, was the guy who ran the local Buick dealership. Every March, he'd come out to the field, unlock the gate, and run a baseball-and-beer operation for the summer. He wouldn't make much money, or lose much either, and he provided professional baseball to a community that would otherwise go without. There's still a bit of this spirit left—I remember one night my general manager at Peninsula proudly told me that he'd found a kid to run the scoreboard and paid him two hot dogs and a Pepsi as wages for the evening's work. This was the kind of business acumen that may at one time have been typical of the minors. But as investing in the minors has become more profitable, it has attracted a more serious crowd. For better or worse—mostly for the better, I think—many of the people in the game today (though certainly not all of them) are very sophisticated businessmen and women who know exactly what they are doing. I don't want to break down the entire world of baseball people into categories, but just to give you some idea of the different kinds of people in the minors, I'd like to offer some portraits of the men and women who work in the game today. Minor-league baseball is still a pretty small club—everyone knows everyone else, and if you invest in this game, you should know these people, too.

The baseball entrepreneur

Miles Wolff, the former owner of the Durham Bulls, and the owner of the most important trade publication in the minors, *Baseball America,* is now setting up a new baseball league with teams in St. Paul, Minnesota; Sioux City, Iowa; Duluth, Minnesota; Thunder Bay, Ontario, and a couple of other cities. It's going to be an independent league, and there's no fee to get in. You have to have enough money to equip a team—but no more than you'd need to start any small business. If the league works, there will eventually be an annual fee imposed to stay in the league, but for the moment, all you need is the credit-worthiness you'd need to get involved in any financial enterprise that requires some capital and some responsibility. (For more on this new league, see Chapter 4.) When Wolff sold the Bulls to Capitol Broadcasting, he wasn't checking out of baseball. He's been in baseball all of his adult life, but he itched to start all over again with something new.

Wolff grew up in a minor-league town, and when he left the Navy in 1971, he signed on as general manager of Savannah in the Class-A South Atlantic League. At that time, he made $600 a month, and the front office consisted of one secretary, who got $70 a week for her efforts. Wolff had various other jobs with other teams, including a couple of stints as a broadcaster, and then, deciding he could do a better job of owning a team than most of the people he'd been working for, bought the Bulls for $2,500 in 1980. At that time, no one outside baseball was interested in owning minor-league teams, and the price was basically the cost of the franchise fee for being a member of the league.

Wolff is convinced that the future lies in the kinds of independent teams he's working on setting up now. He's not at all sorry he sold the Bulls when he did. His feeling is that the revised Professional Baseball Agreement between the minors and the majors will make it harder for the minor-league teams to operate profitably. He points out that there are a bunch of major-league teams for sale right now—maybe as many as ten—and the prices are not going up.

Not everyone, of course, shares Wolff's opinion that the affiliated minor-league teams are a bad place to be at the moment. Although most concede that the big appreciation in the value of these teams that occurred during the 1980s is probably at an end, teams still continue to thrive, and owners and general man-

agers have reason to be optimistic about the future—
despite what the new PBA may bring.

Keith Lupton, formerly the general manager of the
Frederick Keys, a Baltimore Orioles affiliate in the
Class-A Carolina League, is one of the optimistic
ones. Like Wolff, Lupton has been in baseball a good
part of his life, though he started out by turning down
an offer from the Pirates organization when he was in
college. He went back to school, and eventually came
into baseball not as a player but as an owner. He
bought a franchise in the Valley Baseball League, a
summer collegiate league, for $150, which he sold
two years later for $10,000. He worked briefly as a
scout, but hated it. Not that he didn't enjoy finding
talent—and he's a pretty good judge of baseball talent, with the record to prove it—but he despised the
loneliness of the scout's life, moving from one high-
school ball field to another, with no colleagues, no
contact with anyone except the clerk in the hotel.

The Keys are another minor league success story,
bought for $2,500 at the beginning of the decade
(there are three partners who own the team) and
today probably worth around $3.5 million. Frederick
has a good location—according to Lupton, this is one
of the key factors in finding the right team. When they
were the Hagerstown Suns before moving to Frederick in 1989, they were, according to Lupton, off in the
boondocks with no possibility of developing an audience—there just weren't enough people around.
Today in Frederick, they're fifty minutes from both
Baltimore and Washington, D.C., with a home in
Grove Stadium, a modern 5,200 seat facility. Their
fans in those two metropolitan areas have rewarded

them with the largest attendance figures in the league—more than 300,000 people a year pay to see the Keys play ball.

Lupton is a longtime baseball professional—he knows not only the business of baseball, but also the game itself. He knows that his attention has to be concentrated more on what goes on outside the white lines than on what goes on inside. In other words, he's a marketing and promotions expert first, and an expert on baseball talent second.

The general manager

Craig Pletenik, general manager of the Giants' Triple-A franchise in Phoenix, is a man who loves his job. The team moved this year to a brand-new stadium in suburban Scottsdale, where the Giants also have their spring training headquarters. Scottsdale Stadium, reminiscent in its style of Camden Yards, and designed by the same architects, is one of the prettiest little ballparks I've ever seen, and Pletenik is rightly proud of it.

Pletenik has only worked in baseball management for the past five years, but he's been involved in sports all of his life. He came to Phoenix from a job in sports journalism in Texas, taking a job as the public relations man for the Phoenix team. When the then general manager left for another job, Pletenik was on the spot ready to take over. Promotion is at the center of any minor-league operation, and Pletenik's experience was perfect for him to move up.

A general manager, if he knows what he's doing,

keeps his eye constantly on selling the team to the local audience, and that's what Pletenik does. Though he's disappointed that he hasn't been able to provide a winning team over the past few years, he's constantly on the lookout for ways to promote the team to the media and the people of Phoenix. The new stadium has helped enormously—attendance this year set a record—but he feels that until the team starts to win games, the media are going to ignore it. Phoenix has the football Cardinals and the basketball Suns, but their pro baseball team, at least from Pletenik's point of view, gets short shrift from the local papers and broadcasters.

Pletenik grew up in California, and, although he's a New York native, he has the look and laid-back manner of a sun-soaked California boy. We walked around the empty stadium, and he showed me a gadget that must be an exclusive in baseball: a machine that blows a mist of cool water over the fans as they watch their team play in Phoenix temperatures that can still be over 100 even after the sun goes down (needless to say, the Firebirds don't play any day games). When temperature and humidity conditions are just right, the mister works so well that it creates a man-made fog on the field, occasionally becoming so severe that the umpires have to demand that the machine be shut down. It's not unusual to hear the Scottsdale night pierced by chants of "Turn on the mister! Turn on the mister!" from overheated Firebirds fans.

Heat is something a team in Phoenix always has to keep in mind. Pletenik says that he had to resist all impulses to call his team "hot" or write that they were

"really on fire" or any other metaphor that might suggest that it sometimes gets warm in the desert. Everyone knows that it's hot in Phoenix in the summer—
no point reminding them of it.

Pletenik is more interested in promoting his team
to fans than in selling season tickets to corporations
who'll leave their seats empty most nights. In fact, the
skyboxes at Scottsdale Stadium—comfortable air-
conditioned rooms looking out from in back of home
plate—are available to anyone who wants one for
$250 a night, including a pregame meal for the eight
to ten people the box holds. Pletenik calls them "poor
man's skyboxes," and whoever rents one of these for
an evening could give a pretty nice party for a bunch
of friends for a very reasonable price.

Pletenik constantly reminds potential advertisers
that the Firebirds are, all summer long, the only game
in town; that Phoenix is the largest minor-league
baseball market in the country; that attendance has
set records for each of the last three seasons; that the
atmosphere at the stadium is terrific; and that the
signage, public address announcements, sponsorship opportunities, and various kinds of print, radio,
and TV advertising the team sells are a bargain no
advertiser can ignore.

Pletenik points out that Martin Stone, the owner of
the franchise, bought with the plan to make Phoenix
into a major-league city when national-league expansion happened. But his interest in becoming a major-
league owner disappeared when the price of the
expansion teams went up to $100 million. At this
point, he's happy to stay in the minors.

I asked Craig Pletenik what the next step would be

for a man in his position. Was he interested in going up to the bigs? You'd think I'd asked him if he'd like to slam his hand in a car door. Why, he answered, would anyone want to work for a gigantic conglomerate and be a cog in a wheel with a corporate chain of command to report through when you can run a team with four other guys and have the time of your life? When we were leaving the stadium, Pletenik took me over to show me his own office. "You want to see something?" he said. "Take a look at this." He went over to the window of his office, pulled up the shade, and revealed a sight to warm the heart of any baseball fan: right outside the window—the window of the air-conditioned office were he earns his living—is a perfectly manicured baseball diamond, ready for the next game. "How'd you like to go to work in a place like this?" he asked me, gently shaking his head at his own amazing good fortune.

Being a minor-league general manager is not the same as being the general manager of the Oakland A's or the New York Yankees. Bill Blackwell, who's the general manager of the Jackson Generals in the Texas League will tell you exactly what the difference is.

First, he believes in staying in touch with the fans. All owners and general managers, he says, should be walking through the stands, saying hello, and listening to what they have to say. Even if you're running through the stadium to solve some other problem—stop and listen to the customers. Getting to know them is essential to running a good operation. Can you imagine George Steinbrenner walking around saying hello to the guys in the bleachers? Maybe the incongruity of that idea encapsulates in some sense the difference between the majors and the minors.

Blackwell points out that there are a lot of basic hands-on tasks for a general manager—anyone who aspires to this position because he thinks he'll spend the day talking baseball with the manager and the evening having expense-account dinners with local celebrities should probably be looking into another field. A g.m. should walk through the ballpark every day to make sure it's clean—and don't forget to check the bathrooms. Many minor-league owners, as they try to get more women into the park, have discovered that women will inevitably cite as one of the reasons they don't like coming out to the park is that the restrooms are dirty, underequipped, or undersupplied. And I don't think men are fond of filth, either.

Did you check the concessions? Are they set up for the size of the crowd you're expecting? If you run out of beer in the third inning, you're going to have some mighty unhappy fans on your hands—not to mention the lost sales. Did you remember to tell the managers and umpires that you'd like to have a short delay between the fifth and sixth innings while you announce the winner of a promotional contest? Umpires and managers don't like surprises—and it's the umpires who are in charge of the field during a game, not you. Are your park employees in uniform and readily identifiable to the public? Is someone assigned to keeping the restrooms clean during the game? Are your communications to the employees and to the PA announcer in working order?

How about the press and the scouts? Do they have the statistics and rosters they need to do their jobs?

As the game progresses, the g.m. has to be watching everything—his employees to make sure they're friendly, his customers to make sure they're satisfied, his food areas to make sure the lines aren't getting too long, his souvenir stands to make sure they're not running out of inventory. And the whole time he's doing this, he has to be smiling at the fans, talking with them, and listening to their concerns.

When the game, and the post-game promotion if there is one, are done, the g.m. is still working. First, Blackwell says, you should post people at the exits to say good night. Then make sure your post-game summary is faxed to radio stations so that they can use it in the morning. Straighten out the receipts and bank deposits. And since you're the last one to leave, don't forget to turn out the lights.

Not glamorous? Maybe not. But it's this kind of attention to detail that makes a minor-league park the kind of place you want to come back to—and Bill Blackwell is determined to have them come back.

The pioneer

When Leanne Pagliai got a job working as a sales rep for IBM in Peoria, she pretty much figured that she'd be a lifelong IBMer in one job or another. She'd studied marketing in college, and this was the kind of company she'd always intended to work for. But at that time the Peoria Chiefs were the California Angels' Class-A affiliate, and one of the things she liked to do was go out to the ballpark. She even had a boyfriend who played for the team, which made baseball that much more interesting. Still, that was her personal life, and her recreational life—nothing to do with her work life. Time passed, and the boyfriend went out to play for the other Angels A affiliate, the Redwood Pioneers, in California. Leanne was still hard at work for IBM, but she took some vacation time and went out to California. She met the woman who owned the team, and they became friends. She started arranging some promotions for her, doing some TV advertising and other tasks. Pretty soon, she was in love with the business of baseball.

In the meantime, the Midland Angels, the organization's Double-A affiliate had an opening for a sales manager, so Leanne interviewed for the job over the phone, and took it. This would be perfect: the boyfriend's promotion would undoubtedly be to the AA team, and she could move right along with him. Romantic, huh? Well, not quite. As it turned out, the boyfriend got his release from the Angels that spring, and Leanne, in an unconnected development, gave him his release shortly thereafter. But now she was in baseball for good.

There are a few women general managers now—Melody Tucker with the Everett Giants in the Northwest League, Rosie Putnam with Spartanburg in the Sally League—but not many. When Pagliai first came into baseball, it was almost completely a man's world. She remembers going down to the annual promotion conference for minor-league operators in El Paso that first year and being the only woman there besides Karen Paul, who was one of the organizers of the conference. At the 1992 meeting, that room full of good ol' boys looked a lot different.

GREEN DIAMONDS

For the past six years, Pagliai has worked for the High Desert Mavericks, the Padres' Class-A affiliate in the California League (they moved to Adelanto, California three years ago). The Mavericks are a closely held corporation with six stockholders, the most prominent of whom are George and Ken Brett. Pagliai is one of the partners as well. The Bretts own the Spokane Indians in the Northwest League, as well as a minor-league hockey team there.

You would think that in the macho world of professional sports there would be considerable hostility toward a woman g.m., but Pagliai says it's not so. For whatever the reasons, she feels the baseball business is quite accepting of women, and she views the prospect of more women coming into the game with great satisfaction.

Pagliai was once offered a job with the Padres in their promotion department, but she declined. Like many successful minor-league operators, she sees the larger, bureaucratically compartmentalized world of major-league baseball as much less attractive than a small minor-league operation where she's the one making the decisions about every aspect of the team's business. With her full-time staff of seven, her ownership interest in the team, and her love of the business of baseball, Pagliai feels she has found a home in a field she never dreamed of being in when she first started work for IBM.

The businessman

Not all owners grew up in baseball—some made the decision to join the business well after they'd reached the age of reason. And more and more owners have a background in business that serves them well in running a team in the minors. Craig Stein, who owns the Reading Phillies in the Double-A Eastern League, was trained as a C.P.A., and spent two years in the early 1970s pursuing the profession, then a number of years in real-estate development (which he still pursues when he isn't occupied with his Phillies). But he was always interested in sports, and particularly in baseball. He married into a sports family (his father-in-law owned a piece of the Philadelphia Eagles at one time) and when the chance to buy a minor-league baseball team came up in 1986, Stein plunged. His father-in-law knew Joe Buzas, and Buzas was ready to sell the Phillies (which he had picked up for $1 some years earlier). Buzas, of course, also owned (and still does own) several other teams. But he was ready to part with the Phillies. Buzas had a way of doing business that was informal even by the rather loose standards of the minor leagues: he told Stein that one firm contractual requirement was that the contract of sale be no more than three pages long. Buzas is clearly a man who doesn't like to waste time. According to Stein, Buzas didn't even have a lawyer for the deal—I guess he figured he wouldn't need one if the contract was short enough. So Craig had his lawyer draw up a contract in small type with no margins that, in fact, filled only three pages. Buzas signed, Stein signed, and the deal was done. For $1 million, Stein had become what he always wanted to be: a minor-league team owner. Buzas insisted that Stein pay him an additional $1 in cash—that way he could tell his friends in all honesty that he had made a million bucks on this team. As far as I can tell, neither Buzas nor Stein had ever for a moment regretted this deal—Buzas went away richer than he ever dreamed he'd be, and Stein now owns one of the most profitable Double-A teams in the country.

Stein loves baseball, and he loves the baseball business. He's fascinated by the business side, he's an enthusiastic promoter, and he enjoys dealing with the City of Reading, with whom he has a spectacularly good working relationship—something not all owners enjoy with their home towns. Stein's good relationship with the mayor and City Council of the town, he feels, was established at least partly because "I don't have a stick-em-up style." He doesn't rant and rave and threaten to pick up his team and leave every time there's a minor disagreement—he prefers to work things out, and has done so with great success over the years. He didn't go in expecting the city to foot the bill for everything, and the deal he has worked out with the city assures that the city won't go broke supporting him—on the contrary, the city is making money on the team, and so is Stein.

The Phillies and the city of Reading have a deal whereby the city shares in the concession revenue in exchange for maintaining the stadium. Since they have people on the payroll already, it doesn't cost them much to assign some of them to maintenance duty at Municipal Memorial Stadium. Stein spent $350,000 on refurbishing the field and grandstands, and the city chipped in for lighting, a picnic area, and the scoreboard. The whole deal was carried out with respect for the taxpayers' money—and both the city and the team have benefited. I should add that this kind of relationship between the town and the team is not, by a long shot, the general rule in the minors.

The Phillies under Stein have seen five successive years of increasing attendance—in 1992, they had 287,000 people come through the turnstiles. Stein attributes these results to several things. The refurbishing of the park and field was one essential factor—with help from the city, he created a place where people could enjoy watching baseball. He promotes with enthusiasm—every night there's a giveaway, a fireworks display, a show, an appearance by the Phillie Fanatic or the San Diego Chicken, a free totebag, glove, bat, ball—you name it, the Phillies have it, all in the name of giving people one more reason to come out to the ballpark.

Another reason for his success, Stein feels, is the comparison fans draw between Reading and a game at nearby Veterans Memorial Stadium where the parent club plays. The major-league park is only an hour and fifteen minutes from Reading, but it's a world away as a baseball experience. Tickets to the Vet cost an average of about $12. At Reading, it's $4. The souvenir ball that the major-league club sells for $6, is $3 in Stein's place. In Reading, the beer is half the price, the parking is free, the stadium has real grass, and your kid can get a player's autograph without getting a hassle.

The Reading Phillies had revenues of about $2 million last year, of which $800,000 came from concessions. The figure is a little misleading, though, and should not, according to Stein, be taken to mean that he's in the hot dog and beer business. For one thing, a team only keeps about 50% of the gross from concessions—when you sell a ticket you keep 100%. Gate receipts are primary—you have to put people in the seats to make money, and you can't lower the value of tickets by giving them away. He makes some money on advertising sales, both billboards in the field and ads in the program. He also makes a little selling TV and radio broadcast rights, but not much. Broadcasting games, though, is important because it provides publicity and credibility that's hard to come by otherwise. Every broadcast, Stein feels, is a three-hour advertisement for his team and the most valuable product he has to sell: professional baseball.

Stein is a sole owner, an arrangement that's rare today. Most teams are too expensive to be owned by one person—and even if one person can afford it, most people like to spread the risk a little. But Stein says he likes to do it by himself—he doesn't like the idea of being responsible for other partners. He puts large amounts of profit back into the team, and he feels that partners would, quite rightly, demand a greater return on their money than Stein is taking for himself. Of course, he has the luxury—he's successful in another field and doesn't have to depend on baseball for his living. All in all, Stein finds the baseball business a very satisfying way to spend his time, and while achieving a measure of personal satisfaction, he's also been, over the years, one of the most successful minor-league operators.

The visionary

Peter Kirk, whose Maryland Baseball Limited Partnership owns the Bowie Baysox and the Frederick Keys, the Baltimore Orioles AA and A affiliates, has a business card shaped like a tiny baseball, orange stitches printed around his name. I laughed when he handed me one, and he said, "You've got to have some fun in this business, or it's not worth it." Kirk has plenty of fun, but he's serious about baseball, and serious about the future of the game.

For Kirk, the majors and the minors are one organization—the majors may not want to recognize this, but it's true. The minors have flourished over the last ten years by following along with the success of the major leagues, but now the majors are floundering—the buyers of the National League expansion franchises paid, in Kirk's view (and that of most other baseball people) entirely too much for the privilege of being a major-league owner. Now it's the minors' turn to lead the majors back to prosperity.

Kirk feels that fans view the major-league players and owners in much the same way: they see the owners as a bunch of millionaires who don't have a clue about real baseball, and the players as another bunch of millionaires who think it's beneath their dignity to run out a ground ball. Whatever economic implications high salaries or declining TV revenues will have—and they are and will be significant—the real pity of it all is that the joy and fun have gone out of the game as played at the major-league level. It's only in the minors that you find those essential elements.

GREEN DIAMONDS

Kirk says it's time now for the minors to assert that they are an essential part of the business of baseball, not just something for the majors to denigrate on the one hand and exploit on the other. He feels the minors should be taking a leadership role in defining the future of the game—and specifically right now in choosing a new Commissioner. Kirk is a great supporter of the Office of the Commissioner, whatever his reservations about Fay Vincent's performance in that office, and feels it is absolutely essential to have an executive at the top who can, in the well-worn phrase, act in the best interests of baseball. The phrase, for Kirk, is not an empty one. Even though the Commissioner is hired and paid for by the owners, the idea that he can nevertheless insist on independence, be immune from firing, and even impose sanctions on owners is essential. Kirk feels it is important to remember that Fay Vincent was not fired. However great the pressure he was under, he resigned of his own accord, and the principle that the Commissioner cannot be fired by the owners was upheld. For Kirk, this is a distinction that must be made.

Kirk feels the Players' Association has made enormous strides for their members, but in a sense they've done too good a job. The owners and players together have painted themselves into a corner. It's no longer a question of a bunch of zillionaire owners whining because they have to share a few bucks with the players—it has now come to a point where some teams are just spending themselves blind to sign free agents. In the end, Kirk feels, this isn't going to help anyone.

How do you patch up the mess? Kirk is optimistic

that players and owners can sit down and discuss everything: salary caps, compensation tied to performance, revenue sharing. But they'd have to agree to stop playing games with each other, and each side would have to believe that the other was dealing in good faith. Kirk is convincing and knowledgeable, but to most of us, this seems perhaps too optimistic.

Kirk, probably one of the few people in the game who has some historical perspective on the business, has other ideas, too. For example, he sometimes contemplates creating a third major league. When I asked him how you can declare yourself to be a major league, Kirk laughed. "The same way the American and National Leagues did in 1901. They said they were major leagues, and then recognized each other." When you think about it, of course, he's right: the way to become a "major" league is to start calling yourself one and hope others will too.

This would be a league with salary caps, like they have in the NBA. Instead of outlandish free-agent contracts, revenue-sharing would create a system in which players, owners, and the cities and communities that build and maintain parks would all share in the proceeds of the business, instead of being at each other's throats. Maybe, he says, there's a way to make a better major league by starting from scratch.

But all this is of course a long way off, still just an idea inside Kirk's head. Kirk feels that the 1990 PBA agreement, however bad it was for the minor leagues, nevertheless had the virtue of opening up some lines of communication with the majors. He'd like the major leagues to at least allow the minors to be advisors behind the scenes when they choose a new Commissioner, and he's hopeful that they may even formally solicit the views not only of minor-league owners, but of managers, coaches, and players as well.

Appendixes

Appendix 1. Team Locations and Stadium Capacities

ROOKIE LEAGUES

Team and League	Location	Stadium	Capacity
Billings Mustangs Pioneer	Billings, MT	Cobb Field	4,500
Bluefield Orioles Appalachian	Bluefield, WV	Bowen Field	3,000
Bristol Tigers Appalachian	Bristol, VA	DeVault Memorial	2,000
Burlington Indians Appalachian	Burlington, NC	Burlington Athletic	3,500
Butte Copper Kings Pioneer	Butte, MT	Alumni Coliseum	5,000
Danville Braves Appalachian	Danville, VA	Dan Daniel Memorial	2,600
Elizabethton Twins Appalachian	Elizabethton, TN	O'Brien Field	1,500
Great Falls Dodgers Pioneer	Great Falls, MT	Legion Park	3,834
Helena Brewers Pioneer	Helena, MT	Kindrick Legion Field	2,700
Huntington Cubs Appalachian	Huntington, WV	St. Cloud Commons	3,100

183

Team and League	Location	Stadium	Capacity
Idaho Falls Gems Pioneer	Idaho Falls, ID	McDermott Field	3,800
Johnson City Cardinals Appalachian	Johnson City, TN	Howard Johnson	3,800
Kingsport Mets Appalachian	Kingsport, TN	J. Fred Johnson	8,000
Lethbridge Mounties Pioneer	Pocatello, ID	Henderson	3,500
Princeton Reds Appalachian	Princeton, WV	Hunnicutt Field	3,200
Martinsville Phillies Appalachian	Martinsville, VA	English Field	3,200
Medicine Hat Blue Jays Pioneer	Medicine Hat, Alberta, Canada	Athletic Park	2,600
Salt Lake Trappers Pioneer	Salt Lake City, UT	Derks Field	10,184

CLASS A—SHORT SEASON

Team and League	Location	Stadium Name	Capacity
Auburn Astros New York-Penn	Auburn, NY	Falcon Park	3,575
Batavia Clippers New York-Penn	Batavia, NY	Dwyer	3,000
Bellingham Mariners Northwest	Bellingham, WA	Joe Martin	2,200

Team and League	Location	Stadium	Capacity
Bend Rockies Northwest	Bend, OR	Vince Genna	2,850
Boise Hawks Northwest	Boise, ID	Memorial	4,500
Elmira Pioneers New York-Penn	Elmira, NY	Dunn Field	5,000
Erie Sailors New York-Penn	Erie, PA	Ainsworth Field	3,500
Eugene Emeralds Northwest	Eugene, OR	Civic	7,200
Everett Giants Northwest	Everett, WA	Everett Memorial	2,400
Geneva Cubs New York-Penn	Geneva, NY	McDonough Park	2,200
Glens Falls Redbirds New York-Penn	Hamilton, Ontario, Canada	Bernie Arbour	3,500
Jamestown Expos New York-Penn	Jamestown, NY	College	3,324
Niagara Falls Rapids New York-Penn	Niagara Falls, NY	Sal Maglie	1,800
Oneonta Yankees New York-Penn	Oneonta, NY	Damaschke Field	3,500
Pittsfield Mets New York-Penn	Pittsfield, MA	Wahconah Park	5,200

185

Team and League	Location	Stadium	Capacity
Southern Oregon Athletics Northwest	Medford, OR	Miles Field	2,900
Spokane Indians Northwest	Spokane, WA	Interstate Fairgrounds	8,314
St. Catharines Blue Jays New York-Penn	St. Catharine's, Ontario, Canada	Community Park	3,000
Utica Blue Sox New York-Penn	Utica, NY	Donovan	4,500
Watertown Indians New York-Penn	Watertown, NY	Duffy Fairgrounds	3,500
Welland Pirates New York-Penn	Welland, Ontario, Canada	Welland Sports Complex	4,000
Yakima Bears Northwest	Yakima, WA	Parker Field	3,148

CLASS A—FULL SEASON

Team and League	Location	Stadium	Capacity
Albany Polecats South Atlantic	Albany, GA	Banes Sports	4,000
Appleton Foxes Midwest	Appleton, WI	Goodland Field	4,300
Asheville Tourists South Atlantic	Asheville, NC	McCormick Field	3,500

Team and League	Location	Stadium	Capacity
Augusta Pirates South Atlantic	Augusta, GA	Heaton	3,600
Bakersfield Dodgers California	Bakersfield, CA	Sam Lynn	3,200
Beloit Brewers Midwest	Beloit, WI	Pohlman Field	3,800
Burlington Bees Midwest	Burlington, IA	Community Field	3,500
Capital City Bombers South Atlantic	Columbia, SC	Capital City	6,000
Cedar Rapids Kernels Midwest	Cedar Rapids, IA	Veterans Memorial	6,000
Central Valley Rockies California	Visalia, CA	Recreation Park	2,000
Charleston Rainbows South Atlantic	Charleston, SC	College Park	6,000
Charleston Wheelers South Atlantic	Charleston, WV	Watt Powell Park	6,000
Charlotte Rangers Florida State	Pt. Charlotte, FL	Charlotte County	6,026
Clearwater Phillies Florida State	Clearwater, FL	Jack Russell	7,384
Clinton Giants Midwest	Clinton, IA	Riverview	3,000

Team and League	Location	Stadium	Capacity
Columbus Red Stixx South Atlantic	Columbus, GA	Golden Park	6,000
Daytona Cubs Florida State	Daytona, FL	Jackie Robinson Stadium	4,800
Dunedin Blue Jays Florida State	Dunedin, FL	Grant Field	6,239
Durham Bulls Carolina	Durham, NC	Durham Athletic Park	5,000
Fayetteville Generals South Atlantic	Fayetteville, NC	J.P. Riddle	3,200
Frederick Keys Carolina	Frederick, MD	Grove	5,200
Ft. Myers Miracle Florida State	Ft. Myers, FL	Lee Country Sports	7,500
Ft. Wayne Wizards Midwest	Ft. Wayne, IN	Memorial Stadium	6,000
Hickory Rangers South Atlantic	Gastonia, NC	Sims Legion Park	3,200
Greensboro Hornets South Atlantic	Greensboro, NC	War Memorial	7,500
High Desert Mavericks California	Adelanto, CA	Maverick	3,500
Kane County Cougars Midwest	Geneva, IL	Kane County Events Center	3,800

Team and League	Location	Stadium	Capacity
Kinston Indians Carolina	Kinston, NC	Grainger	4,100
Lakeland Tigers Florida State	Lakeland, FL	Joker Marchant	7,000
Lynchburg Red Sox Carolina	Lynchburg, VA	City	4,200
Macon Braves South Atlantic	Macon, GA	Luther Williams Field	3,000
Madison Muskies Midwest	Madison, WI	Warner Park	4,000
Modesto A's California	Modesto, CA	Thurman Field	2,500
Myrtle Beach Hurricanes South Atlantic	Myrtle Beach, SC	Coastal Carolina	3,500
Osceola Astros Florida State	Kissimmee, FL	Osceola County	5,100
Palm Springs Angels California	Palm Springs, CA	Angel	5,185
Peoria Chiefs Midwest	Peoria, IL	Meinen Field	5,750
Prince William Cannons Carolina	Woodbridge, VA	Prince William County	6,200
Quad City River Bandits Midwest	Davenport, IA	John O'Donnell	5,600

Team and League	Location	Stadium	Capacity
Rancho Cucamonga Quakes California	Rancho Cucamonga, CA	City Sports Complex	4,500
Riverside Pilots California	Riverside, CA	Riverside Sports Complex	3,500
Rockford Royals Midwest	Rockford, IL	Marinelli Field	4,300
St. Lucie Mets Florida State	Port St. Lucie, FL	County Sports Complex	7,400
St. Petersburg Cardinals Florida State	St. Petersburg, FL	Al Lang	7,004
Salem Buccaneers Carolina	Salem, VA	Municipal Field	5,000
San Bernardino Spirit California	San Bernardino, CA	Fiscalini Field	3,600
San Jose Giants California	San Jose, CA	Municipal	5,000
Sarasota White Sox Florida State	Sarasota, FL	Ed Smith	7,500
Savannah Cardinals South Atlantic	Savannah, GA	Grayson	8,000
South Bend Silver Hawks Midwest	South Bend, IN	Coveleski Regional	5,000
Spartanburg Phillies South Atlantic	Spartanburg, SC	Duncan Park	3,900

Team and League	Location	Stadium	Capacity
Springfield Cardinals Midwest	Springfield, IL	Lanphier Park	5,000
Stockton Ports California	Stockton, CA	Hebert Field	3,500
Vero Beach Dodgers Florida State	Vero Beach, FL	Holman	6,474
Waterloo Diamonds Midwest	Waterloo, IA	Municipal	5,400
West Palm Beach Expos Florida State	West Palm Beach, FL	Municipal	4,400
Wilmington Blue Rocks Carolina	Wilmington, DE	(Not yet named)	5,500
Winston-Salem Spirits Carolina	Winston-Salem, NC	Ernie Shore	4,260
Winter Haven Red Sox Florida State	Winter Haven, FL	Chain O'Lakes	5,000

CLASS AA

Team and League	Location	Stadium	Capacity
Albany-Colonie Yankees Eastern	Albany, NY	Heritage Park	5,500
Arkansas Travelers Texas	Little Rock, AR	Ray Winder Field	6,083

Team and League	Location	Stadium	Capacity
Binghamton Mets Eastern	Binghamton, NY	Binghamton Municipal	6,000
Birmingham Barons Southern	Birmingham, AL	Hoover Metropolitan	10,000
Bowie Skysox Eastern	Baltimore, MD	Memorial	45,000
Canton-Akron Indians Eastern	Canton, OH	Thurman Munson Memorial	5,760
Carolina Mudcats Southern	Zebulon, NC	Five County	6,000
Charlotte Knights Southern	Fort Mill, SC	Knights Castle	10,000
Chattanooga Lookouts Southern	Chattanooga, TN	Engel	7,500
El Paso Diablos Texas	El Paso, TX	Cohen	10,000
Greenville Braves Southern	Greenville, SC	Greenville Municipal	7,027
Harrisburg Senators Eastern	Harrisburg, PA	River Side	5,600
Huntsville Stars Southern	Huntsville, AL	Joe W. Davis	10,200
Jackson Generals Texas	Jackson, MS	Smith-Wills	5,200

Team and League	Location	Stadium	Capacity
Jacksonville Suns Southern	Jacksonville, FL	Wolfson Park	8,200
Knoxville Smokies Southern	Knoxville, TN	Bill Meyer	6,412
London Tigers Eastern	London, Ontario, Canada	Labatt Park	5,400
Memphis Chicks Southern	Memphis, TN	Tim McCarver	10,000
Midland Angels Texas	Midland, TX	Angels	4,000
Nashville Express	Nashville, TN	Herschel Greer	17,000
New Britain Red Sox Eastern	New Britain, CT	Beehive Field	4,178
Orlando Cubs Southern	Orlando, FL	Tinker Field	5,104
Reading Phillies Eastern	Reading, PA	Municipal	7,000
San Antonio Missions Texas	San Antonio, TX	V.J. Keefe	3,500
Shreveport Captains Texas	Shreveport, LA	Fair Grounds Field	6,200
Tulsa Drillers Texas	Tulsa, OK	Drillers	10,744

Team and League	Location	Stadium	Capacity
Wichita Wranglers Texas	Wichita, KS	Lawrence-Dumont	6,723

CLASS AAA

Team and League	Location	Stadium	Capacity
Albuquerque Dukes Pacific Coast	Albuquerque, NM	Albuquerque Sports	10,510
Buffalo Bisons American Association	Buffalo, NY	Pilot Field	21,050
Calgary Cannons Pacific Coast	Calgary, Alberta, Canada	Foothills	7,500
Charlotte Knights	Charlotte, NC	Knights Castle	10,000
Colorado Springs Sky Sox Pacific Coast	Colorado Springs, CO	Sky Sox	6,000
Columbus Clippers International	Columbus, OH	Cooper	15,000
Edmonton Trappers Pacific Coast	Edmonton, Alberta, Canada	John Ducey Park	6,200
Indianapolis Indians American Association	Indianapolis, IN	Bush	12,934
Iowa Cubs American Association	Des Moines, IA	Sec Taylor	10,500
Las Vegas Stars Pacific Coast	Las Vegas, NV	Cashman Field	9,370

Team and League	Location	Stadium	Capacity
Louisville Redbirds American Association	Louisville, KY	Cardinal	33,500
Nashville Sounds American Association	Nashville, TN	Herschel Greer	17,000
New Orleans Zephyrs American Association	New Orleans, LA		
Oklahoma City 89ers American Association	Oklahoma City, OK	All-Sports	12,000
Omaha Royals American Association	Omaha, NE	Rosenblatt	17,500
Ottawa Lynx	Ottawa, Ontario	Multipurpose Recreational Complex	9,850
Pawtucket Red Sox International	Pawtucket, RI	McCoy	6,010
Phoenix Firebirds Pacific Coast	Scottsdale, AZ	Scottsdale	7,000
Portland Beavers Pacific Coast	Portland, OR	Civic	26,500
Richmond Braves International	Richmond, VA	The Diamond	12,143
Rochester Red Wings International	Rochester, NY	Silver	12,503
Scranton/W-B Red Barons International	Moosic, PA	Lackawanna City	10,776

Team and League	Location	Stadium	Capacity
Syracuse Chiefs International	Syracuse, NY	MacArthur	8,408
Tacoma Tigers Pacific Coast	Tacoma, WA	Cheney	8,500
Norfolk Tides International	Norfolk, VA	Metropolitan Park	6,150
Toledo Mud Hens International	Toledo, OH	Ned Skeldon	10,025
Tucson Toros Pacific Coast	Tucson, AZ	Hi Corbett Field	8,000
Vancouver Canadians Pacific Coast	Vancouver, B.C., Canada	Nat Bailey	6,500

Source: Baseball America

Appendix 2. Ownership of Minor League Teams

Team	Class	League	Owner/Operator	Phone Number
Albany Colonie Yankees	AA	Eastern League	Minor League Sports Enterprises, Inc.	518-869-9236
Albany Polecats	A	South Atlantic League	Albany Polecats Professional Baseball Club, Inc.	912-435-6444
Albuquerque Dukes	AAA	Pacific Coast League	Albuquerque Prof. Baseball Club, Inc.	505-243-1791
Appleton Foxes	A	Midwest League	Appleton Baseball Club, Inc.	414-733-4152
Arkansas Travelers	AA	Texas League	Arkansas Travelers Baseball Club, Inc.	501-664-1555
Asheville Tourists	A	South Atlantic League	Tourists Baseball, Inc.	704-258-0428
Auburn Astros	A	New York-Penn League	Auburn Community Baseball, Inc.	315-255-2489
Augusta Pirates	A	South Atlantic League	Scripps Baseball Group, Inc.	404-736-7889
Bakersfield Dodgers	A	California League	Bakersfield Dodgers Baseball Club	805-322-1363
Batavia Clippers	A	New York-Penn League	Genesee County Professional Baseball, Inc.	716-343-7531
Bellingham Mariners	A	Northwest League	Sports Enterprises, Inc.	206-671-6347
Beloit Brewers	A	Midwest League	Beloit Professional Baseball Association, Inc.	608-362-2272
Bend Rockies	A	Northwest League	Bend Baseball, Inc.	503-382-8011
Billings Mustangs	Rookie	Pioneer League	Billings Pioneer Baseball Club	406-252-1241
Binghamton Mets	AA	Eastern League	Sterling Doubleday Enterprises	607-723-6387
Birmingham Barons	AA	Southern League	Birmingham Barons Baseball Club, Inc.	205-988-3200
Bluefield Orioles	Rookie	Appalachian League	Bluefield Baseball Club, Inc.	703-326-1318
Boise Hawks	A	Northwest League	Diamond Sports, Inc.	208-322-5000
Bowie Skysox	AA	Eastern	Maryland Baseball Limited Partnership	301-791-6266
Bristol Tigers	Rookie	Appalachian League	Bristol Baseball, Inc.	703-466-8340

197

Team	Class	League	Owner/Operator	Phone Number
Buffalo Bisons	AAA	American Association	Bison Baseball, Inc.	716-846-2000
Burlington Bees	A	Midwest League	Burlington Baseball Club, Inc.	319-754-5705
Burlington Indians	Rookie	Appalachian League	Burlington Baseball Club, Inc.	919-222-0223
Butte Copper Kings	Rookie	Pioneer League	Silverbow Baseball, Inc.	406-723-8206
Calgary Cannons	AAA	Pacific Coast League	Calgary Cannons Baseball Club, Ltd.	403-284-1111
Canton-Akron Indians	AA	Eastern League	Canton Professional Baseball, Inc.	216-456-5100
Capital City Bombers	A	South Atlantic League	United Baseball, Inc.	803-256-4110
Carolina Mudcats	AA	Southern League	Carolina Professional Baseball Club, Inc.	919-269-2287
Cedar Rapids Kernels	A	Midwest League	Cedar Rapids Baseball Club, Inc.	319-363-3887
Central Valley Rockies	A	California League	JSS/USA, Inc.	209-625-0480
Charleston Rainbows	A	South Atlantic League	South Carolina Baseball Club, L.P.	803-723-7241
Charleston Wheelers	A	South Atlantic League	DRB Baseball Management II, Inc.	304-925-8222
Charlotte Knights	AA	International League	Shinn Enterprises, Inc.	803-548-8051
Charlotte Rangers	A	Florida State League	Texas Rangers Baseball Club, Ltd.	813-625-9500
Chattanooga Lookouts	AA	Southern League	Engel Stadium Corporation	615-267-2208
Clearwater Phillies	A	Florida State League	The Philadelphia Phillies	813-441-8638
Clinton Giants	A	Midwest League	Clinton Baseball Club, Inc.	708-242-0727
Colorado Springs Sky Sox	AAA	Pacific Coast League	Colorado Springs Sky Sox, Inc.	719-597-2491
Columbus Clippers	AAA	International League	Columbus Baseball Team, Inc.	614-462-5250
Columbus Red Stixx	A	South Atlantic League	Columbus Professional Baseball Club of Georgia, Inc.	404-571-8866
Danville Braves	Rookie	Appalachian League	Danville Braves, Inc.	804-791-3346
Daytona Cubs	A	Florida State League	Anheuser Busch, Inc.	904-257-3172
Dunedin Blue Jays	A	Florida State League	Toronto Blue Jays	813-733-9302

Team	Class	League	Owner/Operator	Phone Number
Durham Bulls	A	Carolina League	Durham Bulls Baseball Club, Inc.	919-688-8211
Edmonton Trappers	AAA	Pacific Coast League	Edmonton Trappers Baseball Club	403-429-2934
El Paso Diablos	AA	Texas League	El Paso Diablos, Inc.	915-755-2000
Elizabethton Twins	Rookie	Appalachian League	City of Elizabethton	615-543-4395
Elmira Pioneers	A	New York-Penn League	Diamond Action, Inc.	607-734-1811
Erie Sailors	A	New York-Penn League	Keystone Professional Baseball Club, Inc.	814-459-7245
Eugene Emeralds	A	Northwest League	Eugene Baseball, Inc.	503-342-5367
Everett Giants	A	Northwest League	Everett Giants, Inc.	206-258-3673
Fayetteville Generals	A	South Atlantic League	Fayetteville Baseball Club, Inc.	919-424-6500
Frederick Keys	A	Carolina League	Maryland Baseball Limited Partnership	301-662-0013
Ft. Myers Miracle	A	Florida State League	Greater Miami Baseball Club, L.P.	813-768-4210
Ft. Wayne Wizards	A	Midwest League	United Baseball, Inc.	219-423-6400
Gastonia Rangers	A	South Atlantic League	George Shinn Sports, Inc.	704-867-3721
Geneva Cubs	A	New York-Penn League	Geneva Clubs Baseball, Inc.	315-789-2827
Great Falls Dodgers	Rookie	Pioneer League	Great Falls Baseball Club, Inc.	406-452-5311
Greensboro Hornets	A	South Atlantic League	Greensboro Hornets Professional Baseball Club, Inc.	919-275-1641
Greenville Braves	AA	Southern League	Atlanta National League Baseball, Inc.	803-299-3456
Hamilton Redbirds	A	New York-Penn League	Hamilton Baseball Associates, Inc.	416-527-3000
Harrisburg Senators	AA	Eastern League	Harrisburg Senators Baseball Club, Inc.	717-231-4444
Helena Brewers	Rookie	Pioneer League	Say Hey, Inc.	406-449-7616
High Desert Mavericks	A	California League	High Desert Mavericks, Inc.	619-246-6287
Huntington Cubs	Rookie	Appalachian League	Huntington Cubs Baseball, Inc.	304-429-1700

Team	Class	League	Owner/Operator	Phone Number
Huntsville Stars	AA	Southern League	Huntsville Baseball, Inc.	205-882-2562
Idaho Falls Gems	Rookie	Pioneer League	Idaho Falls Gems Baseball Club, Inc.	208-522-8363
Indianapolis Indians	AAA	American Association	Indianapolis Indians, Inc.	317-269-3545
Iowa Cubs	AAA	American Association	The Greater Des Moines Baseball Company	515-243-6111
Jackson Generals	AA	Texas League	Cowboy Maloney Supply Co., Inc.	601-981-4664
Jacksonville Suns	AA	Southern League	Baseball JAX, Inc.	904-358-2846
Jamestown Expos	A	New York-Penn League	Montreal Baseball Club, Ltd.	716-665-4092
Johnson City Cardinals	Rookie	Appalachian League		615-461-4850
Kane County Cougars	A	Midwest League	Wisconsin Baseball Partnership	708-232-8811
Kingsport Mets	Rookie	Appalachian League	Greater Kingsport Baseball Association	615-246-6464
Kinston Indians	A	Carolina League	The Kinston Group, Inc.	919-527-9111
Knoxville Smokies	AA	Southern League	Knoxville Blue Jays Baseball Club, Inc.	615-637-9494
Lakeland Tigers	A	Florida State League	Lakeland Sports, Inc.	813-686-1133
Las Vegas Stars	AAA	Pacific Coast League	Las Vegas Stars Baseball Club, Ltd.	702-386-7200
Lethbridge Mounties	Rookie	Pioneer League	Lethbridge Mounties Baseball	403-327-7975
London Tigers	AA	Eastern League	London Tigers Baseball Club	519-645-2255
Louisville Redbirds	AAA	American Association	Louisville Baseball Club, Inc.	502-367-9121
Lynchburg Red Sox	A	Carolina League	Lynchburg Baseball Corporation	804-528-1144
Macon Braves	A	South Atlantic League	Atlanta National League Baseball Club, Inc.	912-745-8943
Madison Muskies	A	Midwest League	Madison Professional Baseball, Inc.	608-241-0010
Martinsville Phillies	Rookie	Appalachian League	Martinsville Phillies Professional Baseball, Inc.	703-666-2000
Medicine Hat Blue Jays	Rookie	Pioneer League	Consolidated Sports Holdings, Ltd.	403-526-0404

Team	Class	League	Owner/Operator	Phone Number
Memphis Chicks	AA	Southern League	PSET, Inc.	901-272-1687
Midland Angels	AA	Texas League	Midland Sports, Inc.	915-683-4251
Modesto A's	A	California League	Modesto A's Baseball Club, Inc.	209-529-7368
Myrtle Beach Hurricanes	A	South Atlantic League	Norwin Corporation	803-626-1987
Nashville Express	AA	Southern League	Nashville Sounds Baseball Club, Ltd.	615-242-4571
Nashville Sounds	AAA	American Association	Nashville Sounds Baseball Club, Ltd.	615-242-4371
New Britain Red Sox	AA	Eastern League	Buzas Enterprises, Inc.	203-224-8383
New Orleans	AAA	American Association	Dikeou Enterprises	504-282-6777
Niagara Falls Rapids	A	New York-Penn League	Niagara Falls Baseball, Inc. of Rich Baseball Operations	716-298-5400
Norfolk Tides	AAA	International League	Tidewater Professional Sports, Inc.	804-461-5600
Oklahoma City 89ers	AAA	American Association	89er Baseball Club of Oklahoma City	405-946-8989
Omaha Royals	AAA	American Association	Omaha Royals, Inc.	402-734-2550
Oneonta Yankees	A	New York-Penn League	Oneonta Athletic Corp., Inc.	607-432-1965
Orlando Cubs	AA	Southern League	Orlando Sunrays, Ltd.	407-872-7593
Osceola Astros	A	Florida State League	Houston Sports Association	407-933-5500
Ottawa Lynx	AAA	International League	Ottawa Lynx Baseball Club	613-747-5969
Palm Springs Angels	A	California League	Quantum Entertainment	619-325-4487
Pawtucket Red Sox	AAA	International League	Pawtucket Red Sox Baseball Club, Inc.	401-724-7300
Peoria Chiefs	A	Midwest League	Peoria Professional Baseball Limited Partnership	309-688-1622
Phoenix Firebirds	AAA	Pacific Coast League	Professional Sports, Inc.	602-275-0500
Pittsfield Mets	A	New York-Penn League	CD&M Associates, Inc.	413-499-6387
Portland Beavers	AAA	Pacific Coast League	Buzas Baseball, Inc.	503-223-2837

Team	Class	League	Owner/Operator	Phone Number
Prince William Cannons	A	Carolina League	Prince William Professional Baseball Club, Inc.	703-590-2311
Princeton Reds	Rookie	Appalachian League	Princeton Baseball Association, Inc.	304-487-2000
Quad City River Bandits	A	Midwest League	Quad City Professional Baseball Club, Inc.	319-324-2032
Rancho Cucamonga Quakes	A	California League	Valley Baseball Club, Inc.	909-481-5000
Reading Phillies	AA	Eastern League	E&J Professional Baseball Club, Inc.	215-375-8469
Richmond Braves	AAA	International League	Atlanta National League Baseball, Inc.	804-359-4444
Riverside Pilots	A	California League	Reno Baseball, Ltd.	909-276-3352
Rochester Red Wings	AAA	International League	Rochester Community Baseball, Inc.	716-467-6732
Rockford Royals	A	Midwest League	Rockford Professional Baseball Club, Inc.	815-964-5400
St. Lucie Mets	A	Florida State League	New York Mets	407-871-2100
St. Petersburg Cardinals	A	Florida State League	Suncoast Baseball Club, Inc.	813-822-3384
Salem Buccaneers	A	Carolina League	Salem Professional Baseball Club, Inc.	703-389-3333
Salinas Spurs	A	California League	SACCI International	408-422-3812
Salt Lake Trappers	Rookie	Pioneer League	Salt Lake Trappers, Inc.	801-484-9900
San Antonio Missions	AA	Texas League	San Antonio Missions Baseball Club, Inc.	512-434-9311
San Bernardino Spirit	A	California League	San Bernardino Spirit Baseball Club, Inc.	714-881-1836
San Jose Giants	A	California League	Progress Sports Management	408-297-1435
Sarasota White Sox	A	Florida State League	Sarasota White Sox, Inc.	813-954-7699
Savannah Cardinals	A	South Atlantic League	Savannah Professional Baseball Club, Inc.	912-351-9150
Scranton/W-B Red Barons	AAA	International League	Lackawanna City Multipurpose Stadium Auth	717-963-6556
Shreveport Captains	AA	Texas League	Shreveport Baseball, Inc.	318-636-5555
South Bend White Sox	A	Midwest League	Palisades Baseball, Ltd.	219-284-9988

202

Team	Class	League	Owner/Operator	Phone Number
Southern Oregon Athletics	A	Northwest League	National Sports Organization, Inc.	503-770-5364
Spartanburg Phillies	A	South Atlantic League	Harrisburg Baseball Club, Inc.	803-585-6279
Spokane Indians	A	Northwest League	Longball, Inc.	509-535-2922
Springfield Cardinals	A	Midwest League	Springfield Cardinals Baseball Club, Inc.	217-525-6570
St. Catharines Blue Jays	A	New York-Penn League	St Catharines Blue Jays Baseball Club	416-641-5297
St. Lucie Mets	A	Florida State League	New York Mets	407-871-2100
St. Petersburg Cardinals	A	Florida State League	Suncoast Baseball Club, Inc.	813-822-3384
Salem Buccaneers	A	Carolina League	Salem Professional Baseball Club, Inc.	703-389-3333
Stockton Ports	A	California League	Joy In Mudville, Inc.	209-944-5943
Syracuse Chiefs	AAA	International League	Comm. Baseball Club of Central N.Y., Inc.	315-474-7833
Tacoma Tigers	AAA	Pacific Coast League	George's Pastime, Inc.	206-752-7707
Toledo Mud Hens	AAA	International League	Toledo Mud Hens Baseball Club, Inc.	419-893-9483
Tucson Toros	AAA	Pacific Coast League	Tucson Toros, Inc.	602-325-2621
Tulsa Drillers	AA	Texas League	Tulsa Baseball, Inc.	918-747-3267
Utica Blue Sox	A	New York-Penn League	Utica Baseball Club, Ltd.	315-738-0999
Vancouver Canadians	AAA	Pacific Coast League	JSS Sports, Inc.	604-872-5232
Vero Beach Dodgers	A	Florida State League	Vero Beach Dodgers	407-569-4900
Waterloo Diamonds	A	Midwest League	Waterloo Professional Baseball, Inc.	319-233-8146
Watertown Indians	A	New York-Penn League	Jefferson County Community Baseball, Inc.	315-788-8747
Welland Pirates	A	New York-Penn League	Palisades Baseball, Ltd.	416-735-7634
West Palm Beach Expos	A	Florida State League	West Palm Beach Expos, Inc.	407-684-6801
Wichita Wranglers	AA	Texas League	Wichita Baseball, Inc.	316-267-3372

Team	Class	League	Owner/Operator	Phone Number
Wilmington Blue Rocks	A	Carolina League	Harrelson Sports Group, L.P.	302-888-2015
Winston-Salem Spirits	A	Carolina League	Winston-Salem Spirits Baseball Club, Inc.	919-759-2233
Winter Haven Red Sox	A	Florida State League	Winter Haven Red Sox, Inc.	813-293-3900
Yakima Bears	A	Northwest League	Tradition Sports, Inc.	509-457-5151

Source: Baseball America

Appendix 3. League Presidents

The President of the National Association of Professional Baseball Leagues is:

Mike Moore
P.O. Box A
St. Petersburg, FL 33731
Phone: 813-822-6937

Here are the names and numbers of the presidents of each of the leagues that are affiliated members of the National Association:

League	President	Address	Phone
American Association (AAA)	Branch Rickey	401 E. McMillan, Suite 550 Cincinnati, OH 45206	513-281-8100
International League (AAA)	Randy Mobley	55 South High Street Dublin, OH 43017	614-791-9300
Pacific Coast League (AAA)	Bill Cutler	2101 E. Broadway Tempe, AZ 85282	602-967-7679
Eastern League (AA)	John Levends	P.O. Box 716 Plainville, CT 06062	203-747-9332
Southern League (AA)	Jimmy Bragan	235 Main Street, Suite 103 Trussville, AL 35173	205-655-7062
Texas League (AA)	Tom Kayser	4068 Tumbleweed Trail Rockford, IL 61111	815-654-9349
California League	Joe Gagliardi	1060 Willow Street 6 P.O. Box 24600, San Jose, CA	408-977-1977

League	President	Address	Phone
Carolina League (A)	John Hopkins	P.O. Box 9503 Greensboro, NC 27429	919-273-7908
Florida State League (A)	Chuck Murphy	P.O. Box 349 Daytona Beach, FL 32115	904-252-7479
Midwest League (A)	George Spelius	P.O. Box 936 Beloit, WI 53512	608-364-1188
South Atlantic League (A)	John Moss	504 Crescent Hill Kings Mountain, NC 28086	704-739-3466 or 487-7264
New York-Penn League (Short Season A)	Bob Julian	P.O. Box 1313 Auburn, NY 13021	315-253-2957
Northwest League (Short Season A)	Bob Richmond	P.O. Box 4941 Scottsdale, AZ 85261	602-483-8224
Appalachian League (Rookie)	Bill Halstead	157 Carson Lane Bristol, VA 24201	703-669-3644
Pioneer League (Rookie)	Ralph Nelles	P.O. box 1144 Billings, MT 59103	406-248-3401
Arizona League (Rookie)	Bob Richmond	P.O. Box 4941 Scottsdale, AZ 85261	602-483-8224
Gulf Coast League (Rookie)	Tom Saffell	1503 Clower Creek Drive, # H-62 Sarasota, FL 34231	
Dominican Summer League (Rookie)	Freddy Jana	c/o Banco Del Progresso Av. John F. Kennedy Santo Domingo, Dom. Rep.	809-565-0714

Index

INDEX

Baxter, John, and South
Bend White Sox, 105,
156–57
Baxter, Rita, advertising
director for South Bend
White Sox, 105–6; quoted,
106
Beer sales, 102–3, 169; and
success of Durham Bulls,
146
Blackwell, Bill, manager,
Jackson Generals,
168–70
Bonus babies, in 1950s, 37
Boone, Bob, 145
Booths, radio and TV, 88
Borrowing, difficulty of,
111–12
Boulton, Frank, investor,
14–15, 17–19; deal with
Wilmington, 86, 92–93
Brett, George, 172
Brett, Ken, 172
Broadcast rights, 43, 113,
176. *See also* Radio
Broken Bat Night, 96–97. *See
also* Promotion
Buffalo Bisons: attendance,
153–54; history, 153;
premium value, 111;
receipts, 95
Burlington Indians, 157–58
Bus trips, 44
Businessmen in baseball,
173–76
Butler, Brett, 145
Buzas, Joe, team owner, 82,
173–74

Campbell, Earl, 101
Canada, conditions for teams,
123
Capitol Broadcasting, 162
Carl, Dave, and Tacoma
Tigers, 99
Carolina League, 145

Carter, Scott, investor, 50–52
Cavanaugh, Jack, *New York
Times* article, 82
Central America, source of
players, 134
Charleston Wheelers, 76, 78;
Noah Night (promotion), 95
Chicago White Sox, 139
Cities: and baseball teams,
87–89, 123, 174–75;
effect of team on
economy, 122–23. *See
also* Local government
Clock, stadium, 89
Clubhouse, 90–91
Coleman, Tom, Mayor of
Albany, Georgia, 86
College baseball, 38–39
College World Series, 150
Colsthen, Fritz, promotion
idea, 96
Commissioner of Baseball:
discussed, 43, 46, 92,
178, 180; major-league
Rule 21, 33; transfer of
control, 112
Concessions: discussed 92,
94–95, 169; hot dogs and
beer, 101–3; lines,
155–56; revenue, 175–76;
sales; 73; stands, 70
Cone, David, 154–55
Conflicts of interest,
unacceptable, 42–43, 113
Control, transfer of: cost, 115;
procedure, 112–14
Corradini, Deedee, Mayor of
Salt Lake City, Utah, 151
Coveleski Stadium, South
Bend. Indiana,106, 127–28

Debt: rule on ratio to equity,
111; service, 73
Derks Field, Salt Lake City,
Utah: attendance, 149;
condition, 151–53

208

Index

INDEX

Index

INDEX